SHEPHERD
of
TIMES SQUARE

SHEPHERD
of
TIMES SQUARE

by
Paul Moore & Joe Musser

THOMAS NELSON PUBLISHERS

Nashville   New York

Contents

Dedication

WHILE THIS BOOK is an autobiography that spans ten years, it is primarily the story of one life that has found itself in the love and lives of others.

This book is lovingly dedicated:

First to my wife Sharon and to our children Sheri, Cathi and Paul II;

to my father and mother, Sartell and Viola Moore, whose tutoring in the things of God and example guided me to personal faith;

and to my church flock, the Lamb's, who fill my life with redemptive purpose and are my fellow pilgrims in becoming whole persons in a broken world.

Preface

SHEPHERD OF TIMES SQUARE is the exciting true-life story of Paul Moore, pastor of Manhattan Church of the Nazarene in Times Square.

Times Square is a study in contrasts, with massage parlors and their prostitutes of Forty-second Street at one end, and the elegant Broadway theaters and their socialite patrons of Shubert Alley at the opposite end. Between these extremes lie just about every kind of business, fashion, or individual. It is the center of power, in entertainment, advertising, television and radio, publishing—as well as in sin. Organized crime, pornography, immorality, satanic cults, and evil influences of every kind are ever present. Christian gains in such strategic areas are made at great personal cost. The casualty rate for workers in this urban mission field are staggering and disheartening.

Paul Moore has chosen to avoid the usual first-person narrative style of an autobiography and its subjective viewpoint. While stories that tell the reader "I saw . . ." or "I heard . . ." or "I did . . ." are sometimes more personal, they quite often blunt the impact. First-person accounts require a sense of modesty, so they can't always tell the full story. Further, first-person accounts aren't always able to give important details about other characters with insight into their thoughts.

Joe Musser (coauthor of the best-seller *Joni*) worked several months with Paul Moore, including many sessions that ran fourteen or sixteen hours a day in dialogue and interviews, to get his story. Musser also questioned other people who are a vital part of Paul's life and this book.

It was our decision to let the reader see for himself how truth often is more exciting and inspiring than fiction. *Shepherd of*

SHEPHERD OF TIMES SQUARE

Times Square is written in novel form. The literary device permits a greater range into the lives, experiences, and insights of the people whose stories intersect with Paul Moore's mid-life autobiography. Using this "omniscient" viewpoint adds unusual drama and suspense.

Paul's story is true. However, a few names and situations have been changed to protect the privacy of certain individuals.

—The Publisher

SHEPHERD
of
TIMES SQUARE

I. Rock and Roll Preacher

 One

THE SOUND ON the recording tape being rewound squealed loudly through the huge studio speakers. The engineer pushed a button on the console and the spinning reels stopped. He pushed another, and the tape reversed and began to play.

In the control room, the producer and soloist listened critically, eyes closed in concentration. It was nearly three-thirty in the morning and if this "cut" was good, the group would end their long session.

In the small studio were several musicians with their instruments. During the playback, they listened with differing reactions. The keyboard man stared into space, his face contorted in what could be either a frown or concentration. The drummer beat a noiseless rhythm in the air with his sticks, keeping time to the recording. The guitar and bass players whispered at the back of the room.

Empty Styrofoam coffee cups were scattered around the studio and control room. Two of the hired musicians were chainsmokers, and the air was blue from their smoke. Cigarette butts, candy wrappers, and the debris from supper added to the litter. Empty Big Mac cartons, bags of half-eaten cold, limp french fries, and sandwich wrappings were scattered on top of the piano, still smelling of onions and pickles.

The soloist nodded his approval when the song ended, and the musicians began to pack up their instruments.

"We'll do a mix-down this afternoon," Paul Moore said. "We need to get some sleep first, though."

Paul was both producer and engineer in the small recording

studio in Queens that he owned in partnership with his friend, Ralph. Paul rotated his head to ease the tension and soreness in his neck. He massaged his tired muscles and stood up. He was an imposing, athletic figure, taller than anyone else in the control room. His facial features were also striking—strong chin and Roman nose, deep-seated, piercing eyes, thick black hair.

Paul, at twenty-six, had been in some facet of the music business since his graduation from high school. Now, he shared his time between the recording studio and his role as pastor of the Maranatha Church of the Nazarene in New Milford, New Jersey.

The big jet plane was about to land at London's Heathrow Airport. While still the middle of the night in New York, the day was well under way in Europe.

Effie Jansen smoothed her hair and designer-tailored suit and waited for the plane to land. The other passengers looked somewhat rumpled, having slept in their seats all night during the trans-Atlantic crossing. But somehow Effie still looked glamorous with her makeup and hairstyle perfect. She drew more than a few stares from the men and women sitting around her.

Effie was oblivious to it all, however. Her mind was busy, thinking about the next few days and what they would bring.

Effie was in London to have an abortion, an operation still illegal in the United States. True, there were doctors in New York who probably would have helped her, but she had chosen this way.

She was still more than a little angry with herself for becoming pregnant. *But these things happen,* she thought philosophically.

Soon it would be over. Another day, a brief surgical procedure, and the unwanted pregnancy would end. It was all very simple—except for what she felt. Inside, her emotions were a complicated jumble. There seemed to be no way of erasing the enormous feelings of guilt that worked on her mind.

But outwardly, Effie appeared totally composed. She smiled

brightly at the business executive examining her from across the aisle.

"I hope you have a productive time in London. Best of luck," Effie said to him as the jet screeched against the asphalt runway and taxied toward the terminal.

〜〜〜〜〜〜〜〜〜〜〜

By four A.M. the musicians had gone. Paul and Ralph shut off the recording equipment and the lights, locked up, and went outside into the chill November air.

"Let's stop off in Manhattan and get something to eat," Ralph said to Paul as they got into the car.

The trip from Queens to Manhattan took only minutes at this time of night, and soon they were in the center of the city. Times Square, just before dawn, was as quiet and as vacant as it would ever be. Yet, in spite of the hour, there were perhaps a hundred people milling around or walking the street.

As the car drove past Rockefeller Center, Paul's mind raced faster than the auto. His thoughts were captured by this city in nearly every waking moment. Manhattan, with its millions of people, was becoming a spiritual concern to Paul.

Ralph swerved to avoid hitting a drunk staggering out from behind a parked truck. The drunks and derelicts were the most obvious street occupants at this hour, although a few out-of-town conventioneers and military men could also be seen.

On Eighth Avenue, quite a few prostitutes still stood on the curb, trying to hook one or two more customers so they could quit for the night. As their car waited at a light, one woman waved flirtatiously at Ralph. She was pretty, with dark brown hair. She wore a short imitation fur jacket over scanty summer attire, despite the cool weather. Her provocative outfit—short skirt, high boots, and tight sheer blouse—were worn to draw stares.

The light turned green and Ralph's car sped away into the predawn night. In a few minutes Ralph and Paul saw the lights of a twenty-four-hour coffee shop and parked.

There were at least twenty people inside, some eating alone, others in small clusters talking and laughing. Two couples in tuxedos, gowns, and furs had apparently been to a party after a Broadway play. Now, they were having a late night snack washed down with plenty of black coffee.

Two nurses sat in a booth passing time before their duty hours began. A security guard relaxed after a night shift at a parking lot. At the counter, two policemen joked with the driver of a newspaper delivery truck. In a back booth, a teenage girl sat with a man old enough to be her father.

Paul and Ralph ate quietly, growing more sleepy with each bite. The sun came up and daylight only heightened the dinginess of the dirty streets outside and the greasy atmosphere inside.

Paul was increasingly moved by the loneliness, hurt, and sickness of this city. Recently an artist-friend had given him an oil painting. It captured a magnificent view of the Manhattan skyline. Paul had hung it in his office and was transfixed by it each day as he used it to focus his thoughts and prayers on New York.

It was almost six A.M. While Ralph lingered over his coffee, Paul went to call home.

"Sharon?" he said quietly into the phone. "I'm sorry I woke you, honey. But we were up all night with the recording session for the J. D. Sumner album. I called to tell you that I'm not coming home. I'm going right to my meeting with Brother White. I'll catch a nap after that at the studio; then we're going to mix-down the album. So, I'll see you tonight. Okay?" He waited for her reply, and then said, "I love you, too, honey. See you later."

Paul replaced the telephone receiver and waved to Ralph. Bleary-eyed from their all-night recording session, Paul was not as sleepy as he should have been. Energized—more by the city and its people than the coffee—he walked with Ralph back to the car. He dropped Ralph off and drove across the river to New Jersey and his meeting with Brother White.

Two

THE REVEREND JACK White glanced at the small clock on the dash as his auto pulled into the parking lot of the Forum Diner on Route 4 in New Jersey.

Jack White, a district superintendent in the Church of the Nazarene, was thirty years Paul's senior and had been a committed churchman all his life. He had risen to the top of his denomination not through political maneuvering, but through exceptionally fine work. He was a man sensitive to God's Spirit, both as a pastor and now as an administrator. He was a man of wisdom and ability, not only a supervisor to Paul Moore but a pastor and spiritual father as well.

He was affectionately called "Brother White" by Paul. "Brother" and "sister" were respectful forms of address in their church, but Paul's respect went beyond formality.

Reverend White pulled into a parking place, and as he turned off the engine, his mind went back to the first time he'd heard from Paul Moore.

〜〜〜〜〜〜〜〜〜〜〜〜

Paul had called Jack White one Monday morning in January, 1969. . . .

"I was in the New Milford church yesterday morning and heard the minister announce his resignation," Paul said.

"Oh?" Reverend White replied. "He hasn't told *me* yet."

Paul continued, "Well, if there's a chance that you'd consider letting me pastor the church, you wouldn't have to pay me. I wouldn't take a salary."

"Are you a minister?" asked Reverend White.

"Uh, no," Paul paused. "But I'm the son of a Nazarene pastor, and I can give you references. I'd like to study and become an ordained minister some day. But meanwhile, I'll keep the church open, hold services, and take care of the building in exchange for use of the parsonage."

Reverend White soon learned that the former minister was to leave in discouragement; and with only a dozen members of the New Milford church left, he would have to consider closing their church. However, after a few days of checking out Paul's references and praying about the matter, Reverend White called back to agree to Paul's suggestion for keeping the church open. He arranged for the nearby Dover Church of the Nazarene—where Paul and Sharon were members and had been married seven years earlier—to issue Paul a local preacher's license and his first preaching credentials. Then Reverend White explained the ministerial self-study program in which Paul would have to enroll to obtain educational and ministerial credentials for eventual ordination. Paul was now the new preacher at the Maranatha Church of the Nazarene in New Milford, New Jersey, a home missions project of the New York district.

From the very beginning this "new" church was unusual, to say the least. It was unlike any other church in the denomination in the sixties. And it was discussed not just in the district, but throughout the denomination.

"There's no explaining it without giving complete credit to God's Holy Spirit!" Reverend White frequently told his superiors from the General Church Board of the Nazarene denomination in Kansas City.

When Reverend White visited Paul's church for the first time he found the building reverberating with the noise of amplified rock music and drums. And if that wasn't enough, the congregation seemed totally out of place because of its lack of traditional decorum. How could worship of God be conducted in such a—he struggled to find the right word; *casual* seemed the best, giving them every benefit—in such a casual place? The church consisted mainly of young people, genuine before God, but exuberant in their praise.

After the service Reverend White admitted to Paul that he had expected something different and unique—but wasn't prepared for what he saw.

"I can't begin to understand what's going on here!" the white-haired man said to Paul, "and I don't like that music one bit! Everything inside me says I should toss you and those rock musicians out of this church! But I can't argue with what's happening here: thirty and forty people coming to Christ every service . . . lines of people to be baptized every week! God is at work. I saw those young people accept Christ, and their decisions were real! I don't understand it . . . but I won't stop it." His words made him sound more like pastor than boss, and Paul began at once to love and appreciate his friend at district headquarters.

In the years since that meeting, the two men had become friends. Paul was sometimes called the "rock 'n roll preacher," but most churches and pastors in the denomination recognized the validity of the New Milford phenomenon and applied the description in a positive sense. There were others, however, who misunderstood his untraditional format and approach. More often than not, Brother White took the brunt of these criticisms.

A genuine revival had begun in New Milford. From an original membership of ten or twelve, the church was to see five thousand people won to Christ.

വാ~ഗ~ഗ~ഗ~ഗ~ഗ~ഗ~ഗ~ഗ~ഗ

Jack White's thoughts returned to the present as he strode toward the lobby of the Forum Diner. He and Paul met frequently at this convenient location and talked church business over coffee.

Paul was already seated in a booth when he arrived, so Reverend White walked over to the table, unbuttoning his topcoat. He laid the coat on the seat as Paul stood to greet him.

Although many years older, Jack White stood straight, though not as tall as Paul who was six feet four. Brother White's handshake was friendly and strong.

The two began their meeting without small talk or preamble.

"Brother White, I believe God may be releasing me from the work in New Milford and calling me to people across the river in Manhattan," Paul told his friend.

"Why do you say that, Paul?" Reverend White asked. "It seems to me that God is very much at work at your church, and you're enjoying a great many spiritual successes. Why would you want to leave now?"

"I'm not sure . . . but every time I drive the streets in Manhattan, I get all torn up inside thinking about all those people with messed up lives trying to cope without Christ. Brother White, we don't have even *one* church for those *millions* of people in Manhattan," Paul said.

"Paul, if God is calling you to New York, He'll make it plain to each of us, when His time is right."

Paul's forehead wrinkled. "I don't understand," he said.

"If you feel God's call to New York," Reverend White told Paul, "there are two things you must do to prepare for such a move. First, we'll have to replace you at New Milford because that work has to go on. Second, we'll have to find the money to start a new work in New York, because we do not have the funds now."

Reverend White put his coffee cup down and dabbed at his mouth with the napkin. "By the way," he said, "speaking of a possible replacement for you, how is your new associate, Charlie Rizzo, doing?"

Paul and Charlie had first met in New Milford when the new pastor had asked Charlie and his rock band to play for a coffeehouse in the church basement. The music was successful in getting the kids to come out to the old frame church, which began to "rock" with the loud music—mostly Beatles' tunes rather than Christian songs because that was all Charlie's group knew how to play.

Every fifteen minutes, between music "sets," "the Rev," as Paul was called by the students, stepped out to present a brief gospel homily. The talk usually tied in with the plaintive lyrics or futile message of the last song and presented Jesus as an answer to life's problems.

Charlie Rizzo was the first to believe and have his life revolutionized by Jesus Christ. The young loser, drop-out, and drug-addict, whose undirected life had no goals, later became the instrument God used to start a significant spiritual revival.

"What is your thinking?" Reverend White asked Paul, bringing him back to the present. "Think Charlie will work out as a replacement some time?"

Paul thought for a moment. Charlie and his new bride, Kathy, were living in an apartment in the church. Paul met with his young protege each day for Bible study, discussion, and discipling. Yet there were still a few rough edges. Paul said, "Well, I really like Charlie, but he's too young and immature in the faith. We can't turn over the work to him. He's not ready."

"Well, I'll have to agree with you," Reverend White said. "Charlie isn't the man for the job just yet."

As the two men concluded their meeting, Paul felt satisfied and encouraged. Brother White again assured him that only finding and training a replacement and raising adequate funding stood in the way of his release from the Maranatha Church in New Milford.

"We'll talk some more, Paul," Brother White said with a smile as they walked toward the cashier. "Keep me posted on this matter. And greet Sharon for me."

Effie Jansen was again airborne, returning from her abortion in London. Although the operation had been a success physically, the experience had left her depressed, sick of life, and searching. Her trip to England had failed to grant her the escape she sought. Landing in the middle of the night at JFK airport, she told herself, "Well, honey, we're back in rough old New York, and you've got to pull yourself together to survive in this town."

Later, a broken ankle confined her to her quiet, lonely room. For nearly two weeks she had time to take inventory of her life. Recalling her Christian mother and upbringing, Effie realized at last that her emptiness was a spiritual problem. She was a sinner who needed to be saved.

Three

SHARON MOORE KNEW her husband would be late for dinner but was grateful it would be one of the last evenings he'd have to work late at the studio. God had prospered the work in New Milford, and so Paul no longer would have to work at two jobs to make ends meet; in fact, Paul was selling the record business in order to devote full time to the church.

Paul had called twice to update her on his schedule since he had awakened her that morning. Now, with rush hour traffic in Manhattan it could be another hour before he would get home. She decided to feed eight-year-old Sheri and little Cathi since they were showing signs of restlessness.

As she stood over the kitchen sink, Sharon felt tired and older than she was. Her figure was not as trim as before the birth of Cathi, and she was quite self-conscious about it. She wasn't overweight, but in contrast to most of the young girls in the church, she saw herself as being somewhat "out of it."

The girls she counselled, however, saw no such "generation gap." Sharon sat through many hours of patient listening and frequently helped desperate young girls who had gotten sick or overdosed on drugs. It was a new generation with problems she had never had to confront, but Sharon never flinched.

At the end of the day, because of the schedule of housework and counselling, Sharon did feel worn out. But she had a deep sense of satisfaction when she watched newly saved, young girls and their boyfriends flushing their marijuana down the toilet in the church basement.

Actually, Sharon was well-equipped for her calling, and so Paul never took her complaints too seriously. When low self-esteem caused her to feel awkward or uncomfortable, he would remind her of her superb qualities and how well she handled herself in contrast to the immature young people around them.

Sharon fed the children and picked at a plate of food herself. After putting a plate of food in the oven to keep it warm for Paul, she cleared the table and went to dress for the evening service. She had just finished fixing her hair and makeup and had slipped into a dress when she heard Paul come in.

As the children abandoned the TV and greeted him noisily, Sharon hurriedly blotted her lipstick and went to greet him herself. Paul kissed her affectionately and asked about her day as he took his plate from the oven. He ate quickly, mentally organizing the evening program as he chewed. In just a few minutes he was finished with both.

"Please hurry, Paul," Sharon urged him.

"Honey, I'm ready. We've got time," he assured her.

Sharon did look tired. Maybe it was the flourescent lighting in the kitchen, but her eyes seemed puffy and red. Her face showed stress and fatigue, even under freshly applied makeup.

"You tired, babe?" Paul asked, gently kissing her cheek once more. "Are you okay?"

"I'm all right," Sharon replied evenly. "How'd your meeting go with Brother White?"

"Fine. Just fine," he said, as he stood. "I guess we better get over to the church."

Maranatha Church was a white colonial building next door to the parsonage. Already a crowd had arrived for the Wednesday night service. After taking the youngsters to the church nursery, Sharon took her place at the piano as Paul rose to begin the service.

Although actually being a pastor's wife was a new experience for Sharon, the role itself was familiar since she had grown up as the daughter of an Assemblies of God minister. Her mother's role as pastor's wife was not unlike her own. Sharon was organist-pianist, church janitor, leader of the women's missionary society, choir director, and Sunday school teacher.

Although Sharon at times resented the "super woman" expectations associated with being a pastor's wife, she never questioned her role and felt spiritually fulfilled by most of what she was doing.

Now seated at the keyboard of the church organ, a new surge of energy and a sense of fulfillment overshadowed her fatigue. Paul, leading the congregation in a hymn, looked over at his wife and smiled warmly, his blue eyes telegraphing his love. Sharon blushed in spite of herself and smiled back. Somehow, everything else was unimportant in this moment. She was radiant and quite beautiful. The tired shadows under her eyes faded and her sagging shoulders straightened. Consciously, at least, Sharon was content.

After the service, she stood beside Paul as the people filed out.

"Great service, Pastor," some would say. "I really appreciated your message."

Paul thanked them, spent time talking with several who seemed to need friendly encouragement, or chatted with one or two who came with a spiritual problem.

Finally, Sharon had Paul to herself. The last of the teenagers had left and Paul came over to where she was waiting. He smiled broadly.

"Let's call it a day, okay?"

They locked the church and, arms around each other, walked next door to the parsonage. She had put the youngsters to bed earlier when Paul was talking with parishioners. Neither spoke as they walked, but warmth and love were communicated without words. Paul had grown to love and appreciate Sharon even more in these days than in the early years of their marriage.

They had married early—at nineteen—but had possessed a maturity that allowed them to defy the bad odds of "young" marriages.

Paul had grown up as the only son of a Nazarene preacher, Reverend Sartell Moore and his wife, Viola. He loved his father and was influenced by his values and goals. His dad had lived what people defined as a "wholly sanctified" Christian lifestyle. Paul was to become his dad's best friend. Whenever a church member asked Reverend Moore to go on a fishing trip, Paul's dad would reply, "Sure. I'd like to go. But is it all right with you if I take my boy with us? I really don't think I'd like to go without my son. Is that okay with you and the other fellas?"

But it was more than this companionship that rubbed off from Sartell Moore onto his boy, Paul. When his dad had a wedding, young Paul sat on the pew near the front. When Reverend Moore conducted a funeral, the boy frequently rode in the car with his father to the cemetery. Evenings, young Paul would linger in the study as his dad prepared his Sunday sermons. Without realizing it, young Paul was being trained for a task God would call him to twenty years later.

From his father Paul received a rich background in sermon preparation and preaching. It was a heritage that he simply never could have received from books. Paul was tutored in the things of God, and God would one day call him to preach as He had called his father.

As a teenager, Paul was happiest at church music gatherings. One night, at an "all night gospel sing," Paul talked a travelling gospel quartet into letting him book a concert appearance for them. He was eighteen years old and just out of high school. He became a talent booking-agent and set up a series of such events.

In fact, it was during this time that the young entrepreneur met Sharon. She was president of the Assemblies of God youth group and a top seller of his concert tickets.

Sharon was vivacious and outgoing. Blue-eyed with blonde hair, at nineteen Sharon had a softness, sweetness, and radiance that completely captured Paul's heart. She had an intuitive sensitivity to other people, coupled with a creative and artistic spirit. Before long Paul was ardently in love with Sharon, and asked her to be his wife. They were married nine months to the day after their first date.

Perhaps Paul was thinking of these earlier romantic moments as he and Sharon walked arm-in-arm. But he said nothing.

As soon as they crossed the threshold, for Sharon the mood broke. The dishes needed to be put away. Clothes had to be folded. Diapers needed to be laundered. There were dozens of reminders that she was chained to unending responsibility.

Perhaps it was the late hour, the accumulated strain of the day, or the long list of unfinished duties, but Sharon was suddenly aware of a developing tension headache.

Its cause, no doubt, was the never-ending demands of her roles as housewife, mother, and pastor's assistant. In fact, only recently had Sharon's two years of care for Paul's dad ended with his death from cancer.

"Aren't you coming to bed?" she asked Paul.

"In a little while. I've got some final paperwork to do for closing down the record company."

The record company was an outgrowth of Paul's involvement in the concert ministry. At first he had only booked talent. Then he had started a record label and begun to produce custom record albums, mostly for churches and gospel musicians. It was a moderately successful enterprise, even though at this time the demands of Maranatha Church had reduced Paul's involvement in the company to a minimum.

The recording enterprise had really begun as the result of a Thanksgiving family gathering nine years before. Paul and Sharon were at her parents' home along with Sharon's sister Joanne, and her brother Don, and his wife Ruth. It started out as simple fun with the usual singing—then they began imitating some of the popular recording groups, mimicking their style and sound. It sounded pretty good to them. Later that day, when a local pastor stopped by and overheard them, he went into the living room to compliment the young singers.

"Wow! I didn't know Reverend Storms had such a great music group in his family. Are you booked for New Year's Eve? I'd like to have you sing at our watch night service!"

That marked the beginning of the King's Key Notes, and soon after they went on the road full time. Paul booked the group in churches and auditoriums—some three hundred one-night concerts each year—over the next five years. Little Sheri Dawn travelled with them from the start. By the time she was two, Sheri was singing before large crowds with no shyness or stage fright. They put over four hundred thousand miles on a Greyhound-type bus and recorded thirteen albums. It was in producing their second album that Paul and his brother-in-law Don decided to launch the record company.

Four

GETTING BACK INTO the discipline of academic work at Bible college was hard at first for Bob DiQuattro, an energetic Italian who was Paul's friend and with his wife had once been a member of the King's Key Notes. But he was glad to be back in school, recalling his first year there, some six years earlier. His memories were bittersweet.

◦◦◦◦◦◦◦◦◦◦◦◦◦

It was the year Bob asked Esther to marry him. Both were Christians and felt God had brought them together, although her mother was trying to discourage their marriage. Esther and her mother had started attending meetings at the home of an unusual woman, a self-styled "prophetess" of "The Fellowship," as the group members called themselves. The prophetess commanded a loyalty that seemed diabolical to Bob. She exerted an unusual power over those in attendance. In one of her "prophecies," she had told her followers that God would frown on any marriage between a person in the group and an outsider. This obviously applied to Esther and Bob, and they knew sexual abstinence would be required of them. Bob thought they had surrendered their minds to the prophetess.

In a moment of tense anger, Bob tried to convince Esther that their loyalty and worship belonged to God only.

Esther was totally confused and frightened. She had been taught to respect her parents and church authority. Bob was asking her to reject the prophetess and her cult-like following, and in so doing, disobey her mother.

"I . . . I can't!" she sobbed to Bob.

"But we don't have any life—any future—like this," Bob pleaded tenderly. "They aren't following the Bible. They're trying to brainwash you!"

"But I can't disobey my Lord either," Esther cried.

"You're old enough to make your own decisions. You're an adult. Think of yourself, of *us*!"

"No . . . I can't do it! I'm sorry Bob. We have to break our engagement. I love you, but it's *wrong* for us to get married, don't you *see*?"

"What I see is a very confused young woman," Bob said sternly, and he left.

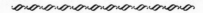

Six months after the parting, Bob received a telephone call.

"Bob . . . it's me, Esther."

"Yes?" Bob replied, his heart beating faster.

"Bob, if you still want to get married, I'm willing to go ahead," she said softly.

Although there were 250 miles between them, it did not take Bob long to respond. Within a few weeks they were married, with the promise of living "happily ever after." Or so Bob had hoped.

Now, four years later, as Bob returned from classes, he was little prepared for the bitter turn his life was about to take. A note from Esther awaited him. Stunned, Bob learned that after their years of marriage, Esther believed that she was out of God's will for having married him and felt compelled to go back to New York to the Fellowship and make things right.

For nearly a week Bob waited with no word. Finally, a call came from Esther. She sounded like another person.

"I'm going to stay here in New York to be with the Fellow-ship."

"But . . . ," Bob tried to interrupt.

"If you want to, you can move here. But my mind is made up."

Abruptly there was a disconnection. Bob agonized over what to do for a long time and then decided that if he wanted to keep his wife, he would have to drop out of college again and move to New York. He didn't know that even moving would not get her back.

 Five

IN NEW MILFORD, an extraordinary movement of God's Holy Spirit was about to take place. Initially, Paul had become pastor of the church to keep it open and take advantage of its free housing opportunity. He discovered, however, that he had a gift for preaching, which had been quietly learned in the shadow of his father. The congregation was beginning to grow in size and spiritual commitment. Through it all, Paul watched in amazement, almost as a bystander. He knew that he lacked the spiritual maturity and depth of his father. His sermons were traditional and doctrinally correct. Yet, they were not based on the reality of personal experience.

This gaping lack bothered Paul increasingly as God convicted him about it. The Lord was working in the lives of some in the church, but more often than not *in spite of* rather than *because of* Paul.

One Saturday night while preparing for a sermon, Paul became even more bothered about his hypocritical attitude and lifestyle. He and others in the church had deluded themselves into thinking that "echolalia"—the parroting of the proper "thou shalt nots" and quoting the right Bible verses—was enough to maintain spiritual faith and religious piety.

Paul spent a sleepless night reflecting on his ministry. True, there were "results" that had deluded him into thinking all was right. The coffee house was always filled and there had been a nominal increase in church attendance on Sundays. The Sunday school was growing. A few, like Charlie Rizzo, had been saved, but there had been no real outpouring of God's Spirit.

At four in the morning, Paul was still wrestling with the issue, recalling his Wesleyan heritage and the words of the apostle Paul, "Have you received the Holy Spirit since you first believed?" This thought echoed again and again. It was as if his heart hungered for his own personal Pentecost—the kind of experience he preached that others needed, but which he now saw was missing in his own life.

Paul at last saw himself standing in the way of God's Holy Spirit. "Not I, but Christ," he prayed—not as before, a pat phrase bordering on triteness—but now a heartfelt prayer to be "delivered from self." He fell asleep thinking about the sufficiency of Christ to meet all of life's basic needs. "Simply Jesus . . . more of Jesus . . . let me know more of Christ," he prayed as he finally dozed off.

After a few refreshing hours of sleep, Paul awoke to take his thoughts into the pulpit. His theme about the power of the Holy Spirit to energize and sanctify came alive in his sermon. When he ended his message, Paul invited his listeners to come to the altar and be filled with the Holy Spirit—to have the entirety of their beings sanctified wholly by Him.

Reverend Paul Moore was the first seeker to come, weeping and earnestly asking God's forgiveness. In a beautiful moment of repentance followed by a deep inner assurance of pardon and peace, Paul surrendered completely to the Lord.

Soon New Milford was having two Sunday morning worship services. The tag "hippie" church was only fairly accurate. A few were drop-outs or drug "crazies," but the majority of converts were young people between thirteen and thirty who were disillusioned with life in general and organized religion specifically.

Charlie Rizzo, the talented guitarist-composer who was the first convert, now had a desire to make music for God's glory. He wrote several songs about his changed lifestyle. During the evening meetings at the coffee house, he performed these songs with deep meaning and emotion. Often tears would stream down his face after singing or speaking about his past and God's salvation for him.

Six

FAR AWAY FROM the noise and dirt of New York City, twenty-one-year-old Barbara Billings stood in a quiet autumn woods in New Hampshire. Somehow the pastoral setting made her feel close to God. *God.* The word had no personal meaning to her. It was a word she used to give order and symmetry to the universe. *Take these woods, for example,* Barbara thought. *Nature has some kind of grand plan that makes it all fit together. The trees and plants contribute to the squirrels; everything has balance and purpose. Except me,* she mused.

Not many people would have agreed that anything was missing in her life. Barbara had grown up in a typical middle-class New Jersey suburb. She attended a fashionable denominational church and found the Sunday services to be beautiful and inspiring. But her faith was more sentiment than belief. Having graduated from Elmira, a prestigious eastern college, four months earlier, she still had a feeling that something was missing in her life.

Actually, Barbara was one of an entire generation in search of personal meaning. Many young people had turned their backs on family, church, and school to pursue some abstract dream or "higher state of consciousness" in drugs, sex, or strange religions—like the kids who shaved their heads, donned saffron robes, and sought some measure of sense in chanting on street corners. Barbara could never understand what these religious fanatics had found so meaningful, but neither were sex nor drugs "her thing." It seemed to her that reality, not escape, was what she sought.

For a while, Barbara thought she might find that "unknown something" within herself. She studied and practiced Trans-cendental Meditation in New Hampshire. She got involved with TM not so much for its religious purposes, but because its proponents told her she would gain new energy, inner guid-ance, and peace of mind through it. But to Barbara, the whole thing became boring.

Yet the needs in her life were still too abstract to verbalize. She really didn't know what she was looking for herself, so how could she ask others how to find it?

Barbara sighed deeply and watched a squirrel busy burying acorns some twenty yards from where she stood.

ᗆᘓᗆᘓᗆᘓᗆᘓᗆᘓᗆᘓᗆᘓᗆᘓ

"Hello . . . my name is Effie Jansen," the caller said. Her voice, even over the telephone, was smooth and satiny. Paul listened to her story.

"I'm a night club entertainer. I sing and play in Manhattan clubs—songs about people falling in and out of love, mostly," Effie explained, telling how until recently she had been living a pretty uninhibited lifestyle . . . marijuana, pills, liquor. And her priorities had been all wrong—"like sex, material things, and myself were the most important aspects of life," she admitted. "But now I'm a new Christian."

"My mother just passed away, and I went home to Denver for her funeral. And while I was there, I went to a Barry McGuire Jesus concert and got saved. It was there that I picked up a flyer listing the Maranatha Church in New Milford. I'm calling to find out more about your church," Effie told Paul.

"Well, why don't you come on Sunday and see for yourself," Paul suggested. He went on to invite her to come and meet some of the group at a rehearsal they were having in New York City for a "Jesus Rally" concert.

The next day Effie stopped by the studios where Paul and the Maranatha Band were preparing for a New Year's Eve concert and communion service at Carnegie Hall. There was an audible gasp as soon as she walked in. In contrast to the casual dress of the musicians, Effie walked into the room with such style and grace that everyone turned to notice. Dressed in a long black gown, mink coat, and ostrich feather boa, she was the epitome of style and elegance. In spite of her recent conversion and the fact that she was now a spirit-filled believer, Effie had kept her own uniqueness.

 # Seven

JOE COLAIZZI SAT behind a desk in the radio-TV department of Pittsburgh's Carnegie-Mellon University. Colaizzi, slender and dark, was director of the department, although he looked more like a student. Rough-featured but good-looking, he sat alone, shaking and then weeping quietly. His mind drifted in and out of reality. He was having another drug "flashback." They seemed to be coming more frequently now.

Joe Colaizzi had graduated from the University of Cincinnati with a degree in radio and television communications. He and his sweetheart, Dolly, had married but had slowly drifted apart until finally she divorced him, perhaps because of his drug habit.

As Joe sat at his desk, he desperately wished he could get control of himself. In his stupor-like condition, the young director reached into his desk drawer, his hands shaking, and desperately searched for the small green bottle he kept inside. He tore at the cap and several red and white capsules spilled out.

Colaizzi's mind struggled with his mental fog. He somehow

sensed that the marijuana, instead of giving him the "high" he had sought, had betrayed him again. His mood was depressive, paranoid.

It was during these times he was reminded that he was Satan. In his more alert moments Colaizzi knew it was the drugs "speaking." Yet, now there was a deep reality to his conviction. He didn't know how he had *become* Satan—he just knew that he was.

He swallowed one of the capsules, not bothering to find water to wash it down. It caught in the back of his dry throat and he gagged. A moment later he was vomiting into his wastebasket.

He cleaned up and went home to his small studio apartment just off campus. It was as dark and depressing as its occupant. Occult books and posters dominated the room along with a few religious pictures and relics, perhaps carry-overs from his strong Roman Catholic background and a childhood steeped in parochial school education. On one wall was a plaster crucifix. On another, by his bed, was a "pop" poster depicting Jesus in contemporary counter-culture garb. Its caption declared, "It's okay with me if you wear long hair."

Joe ran into his bathroom and turned on the light. What he saw in the mirror frightened him. *It was Satan*—he knew it now!

Somehow Satan has taken over my body as well as my soul! he thought. *I'm the incarnation of the devil!* The idea both revulsed and energized him. *It would be best if I killed Satan!* Colaizzi told himself.

He had thought of suicide before but had never been able to find the nerve. Now he wondered if he had the resolve he needed, and the strength. If he did, it would be over soon, and his suffering would end.

However, some unknown force seemed to keep him from following through with self-destruction. Even this hesitancy to end his life added to his confusion and anger.

"Dammit! Can't I do *anything* right?" he shouted to himself. He turned and faced the wall of posters in the room. It seemed to his tormented mind that the poster of Jesus was suddenly a window and not a drawing. He imagined himself looking at Christ for the first time as a real Being.

Colaizzi sank to the floor beside his studio bed. His mind was still under the influence of drugs, but a small spark of clarity was within him somewhere, somehow.

He was stoned and bawling like a baby, but Joe heard himself cry out in desperation and genuine recognition. "Jesus! Jesus— if You're real, Man—You've gotta do something in my life! Jesus, do You hear me? I need help!"

Eight

B Y THE SPRING of 1972, the New Milford Church of the Nazarene was a success by anyone's standards. Thousands of young people had been converted and redirected through Paul Moore's ministry. Both he and the church had earned a national reputation of being responsible, humanly speaking, for the beginning of the East Coast's Jesus Movement. *Time* and *Newsweek* had extensively covered the nationwide movement among young people and some of the people behind it. Several New York television stations and a network TV crew had helped make the movement a media event—with both positive and negative results. CBS-TV, featuring Paul and the New Milford story, aired the program on coast-to-coast television on *Lamp Unto My Feet.*

On the bad side, comments and film clips were sometimes edited indiscriminately, with quotations given out of context in order to sensationalize what was happening. For the most part, however, Paul had learned to use that technique in his favor. He mentally organized his thoughts before most interviews and made statements that were clear and would be able to stand alone if some TV director cut all but twenty seconds from the tape.

Paul's comments were succinct, provocative, and specific. The press and TV people were not able to dismiss the nationwide religious revival among young people as simply another fad—like the long hair, outlandish dress, drugs, and other "counterculture" lifestyle elements.

The Jesus Movement, which on the East Coast began at New Milford, reached a high point with a huge "Jesus Rally" on April 16, 1972, at Carnegie Hall. Charlie Rizzo and his Maranatha Band were featured along with other Maranatha Church musicians converted during the revival. Danny Taylor, whose music was exceptionally popular with the youthful crowd, was the main attraction, along with Andrae Crouch and the Disciples. A sold-out crowd jammed the famous auditorium, and nearby Calvary Baptist Church was filled with the overflow audience. It was a moment of celebration for the thousands of young people who had found new and revolutionary life in Christ.

ᗡᗴᗡᗴᗡᗴᗡᗴᗡᗴᗡᗴᗡᗴᗡᗴᗡᗴᗡᗴ

Paul worked diligently to prepare his way for leaving the New Milford Church. Once in a while, he had to go to Manhattan, irresistibly drawn to the streets depicted in the skyline painting on his office wall.

Sharon understood when he told her one day, "Honey, I need to drive through Manhattan with my cassette tape recorder and capture the spirit of the city as we prepare to go there."

She did not tell him of her inner fears about moving to New York. Instead, she encouraged him with a lingering kiss and sent him on his way.

For some reason, traffic going into Manhattan was light that day. Paul drove down the West Side Highway and breezed into the city. He drove up and down the streets. He saw things he had seen hundreds of times before, but today he saw them with new sensitivity.

Drunks wandered aimlessly from bar to bar as Paul crossed onto Forty-fourth Street. He turned the car onto Broadway and saw the thousands of grim-faced commuters hurrying home and early evening patrons rushing to the theaters. Occasionally an old derelict or "bag lady" went by, their slow-paced movements on the sidewalk a bizarre counterpoint to the breakneck pace of others. He neared Times Square and turned onto Forty-second Street. Here he saw the porno and "live sex acts" theaters. Massage parlors, adult book stores, and similar pornographic establishments were the majority of businesses in the area. What had once been a national tourist attraction was now a sleazy and sinful cesspool of human perversion. Movies advertised not merely graphic sex, but copulation between homosexuals, animals—and the latest perversions—sex with children and violent murder during the sex act on screen.

Paul was aware of such perversity, as were most New Yorkers by now. Yet as he drove these streets, he was suddenly overwhelmed with feelings of concern for the people walking them. He was also more aware, now, of how God must feel at the thought of how badly some of His created children have fallen. Paul began to weep as he continued to drive through Manhattan's East Side.

He drove past the singles bars—Adam's Apple, Noah's Ark, the Tittle Tattle Club, and dozens more. He knew that every evening these were packed with businessmen, secretaries, sales people, actors, models, accountants, and clerks. Most of them were single or divorced, between twenty and thirty-five. They all had a common denominator—loneliness. It was ironic that so many could be lonely in a city of millions. Yet, loneliness brought them to the clubs and bars. They hoped to meet someone with whom they could talk or begin a relationship. Usually, however, the best one hoped for was not to go home alone. Going home alone meant failure. Even a one-night sexual contact was better than going home alone.

Again, Paul was touched with the despair these singles bars represented with three hundred thousand singles and career couples within a few blocks.

"Lord," he prayed aloud, "release me from New Milford so I can come to Manhattan and start a church here. There is so much need, God; I'm feeling a little bit like You must feel. Please, Lord . . . I want to work for You here. When I meet with

Brother White again, Lord, confirm in *his* heart my calling. Lead us to the funds we'll need . . . find us a place to meet and worship . . . and please reassure Sharon's heart about moving."

Paul stopped to call Sharon. He wanted to tell her again of his vision. The more he talked with her, the more excited he became. "We'll start a church right here in Manhattan! We'll begin with the singles, then work into other areas—theater people, the derelicts and bag ladies, the junkies, the socialites in their town houses. It's a fantastic mission field and I'm really excited! Just think about it . . ." he told her.

Sharon couldn't share in his enthusiasm fully. For the moment, she could only think of her lovely two-story suburban home, now completely renovated and decorated in the fashion that she had wanted for several years. Sharon didn't know if she wanted to give up the quiet, tree-lined streets for the uncertainty and threats of New York City. Sheri was in a safe suburban grade school and Cathi was ready to enroll in kindergarten. *Where and how would they go to school in Manhattan?* Sharon wondered.

As Paul continued talking about his dream, Sharon thought of the difficult struggles during their early days in New Milford. They had once labored for little or no salary, and only recently had things gotten to the place where they were somewhat secure. The church was able to support them financially, and Paul's company, Celestial Records, which before had kept her husband away from her and her family, was only a memory. It seemed foolish to her to think of leaving New Milford.

Deep inside her, she struggled to find peace. She did not *want* to go, and she honestly expressed her feelings to Paul on the phone. "I just can't get as excited as you are, Paul. I'm scared. But God has called us to be together; and if He wants you in Manhattan, I'll go . . . and it'll be okay. But just be patient with me," Sharon said. "Give me some time to catch up with you."

Before they hung up she thought to remind him, "Oh, by the way, the producer of the *David Susskind Show* called. He wants you to call him back. Here's the number."

 Nine

TWO WEEKS AFTER Paul's visit to New York, a sales clerk in the fashionable Saks Fifth Avenue looked out the store window toward Saint Patrick's Cathedral across the street. There was a small group of young people sitting on the steps. One was playing a guitar and the others were singing. A crowd had gathered to listen. Maggie could not hear their music and was curious about them.

When it was time for her break, Maggie slipped on her coat and walked across the street. The singers were dressed in jeans and long dresses. Their long hair and beards immediately identified them as not being from the mainstream of society, but their music wasn't as easily categorized. Maggie recognized one or two older hymn tunes, including "Amazing Grace," but the other songs were new to her. During a pause she asked one of the girls who they were.

"We're from the Maranatha Church in New Jersey. We came here with our pastor tonight to tape a TV show," the girl explained.

"Really? What TV show?"

"The *David Susskind Show.* I guess it's going to be about the Jesus Movement."

"And you guys all go to that church?"

"Uh-huh," the girl nodded.

"Sounds interesting," Maggie replied, suddenly wishing there was a church in Manhattan like that—one that appealed to her generation with its different tastes in music and dress but with the same thirst for God as that of previous generations. Maggie did not go to church regularly, although lately she had felt an increasing desire to look into "this whole God thing," as she had told one of her friends recently.

Although she seldom watched television, Maggie found herself tuning in to the *David Susskind Show* when it was broadcast later. After seeing the group once more, this time with their energetic and articulate young pastor, she more than ever wished there was a church like that in Manhattan.

Maggie knew this was the beginning of a genuine search to find God, to have in her life and experience what these young people had found. She knew she would not be satisfied until she found that same quality for herself.

On the night of the *David Susskind Show* telecast, others were watching as well. In Connecticut, at Yale University's Divinity School, two students were trying to watch some TV after studying.

Joel Tucciarone fiddled with the ancient Dumont set, trying the rabbit ear antenna in various positions. The snowy picture on the small round tube was hardly distinguishable.

"You might as well give up, Joel," his roommate said. "It's impossible to pick up New York on that old clunker."

Joel clicked the tuner around the dial, and each channel was too blurred for them to see a picture. Joel stopped at channel five. To his surprise, the signal was coming in clearly. It was the *David Susskind Show* featuring the young people from Maranatha Church. Also featured was evangelist Arthur Blessitt who had gained media attention by carrying a huge cross from city to city.

The two students looked at each other with astonishment.

"Maybe the Lord wants us to see this program so we can pray for others watching," Joel said. So they began to pray that God would use the words of the evangelist and minister to bring many people watching to Christ.

They finished praying and looked up to see Blessitt hold up his Bible and look from Susskind directly into the camera.

"This book has the power of God behind it," he said simply.

On a thirty-two-foot yacht headed out to sea, only one person was aboard. Half-drunk and completely disillusioned with life, the young captain figured he would take his ship out to sea and not return.

David was the son of a successful minister. He had grown up in the parsonage, hearing his father preach the values David had since come to despise. In his early years he had made a commitment to Jesus Christ. Through the years, however, David had become what his preacher-father called "backslidden." There hadn't been a specific time when David said he was going to throw out all the values and Christian principles of his early years. It simply happened that in moral matters he had chosen to "do his own thing," and "his thing" was often in contradiction to church teaching.

Sex, liquor, drugs, and other escapist activities could not completely erase his earlier convictions, however. Deep inside, David knew the distinction between right and wrong. Perhaps the line was different for someone else, but as his father's son—he *knew*. He could not live with the guilt, yet his pride kept him from making things right.

He wasn't certain if he would actually commit suicide out there in the middle of the Atlantic. With winter approaching, he might not have to, he reasoned. A storm could make quick work of his thirty-two-foot cruiser and of him as well. That seemed to suit David just fine, and he gunned the engine as he headed his craft across Raritan Bay out to sea.

Mindlessly, he had been watching television. Now he was fascinated by the tube. It was a talk show with a familiar host, although he couldn't remember the name. It was an interview with some men discussing the religious revival among young people.

"There's no stopping the Spirit of God," one of the ministers was saying. Then, almost as if he interrupted his train of thought, he turned and spoke directly to David.

"This book has the power of God behind it," he said, pointing to his Bible.

The remark instantly sobered him. He felt a rush of air go out of him as if he had received a blow in the solar plexus.

"This book *is* the Word of God," the speaker continued. Another sudden rush came over David, except this time a jumble of Bible verses that he had memorized as a child poured from some deep inner recess of his mind. Even the archaic prose of the King James Bible cut through his drink-clouded brain into sharp focus. He had instant understanding of those memorized verses. Try as he might, he could not dismiss them from his consciousness.

For all have sinned and come short of the glory of God. . . .
For by grace are ye saved through faith. . . .
Draw nigh unto God and He will draw nigh unto you. . . .
. . . put away lying. . . .
Flee fornication. . . .
. . . grieve not the Holy Spirit of God. . . .

There was no escaping. God's words and thoughts were permanently embedded in his brain and could never be erased. Many times before, a verse or two from his subconscious would arrest his conscious thoughts, but never had so much tumbled across his mind in this way. It overwhelmed him. It stopped him.

David turned the big boat around. When he got back to the harbor and dock, he would telephone his father. It was time to surrender to Christ, this time for good.

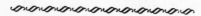

Barbara Billings was in Chicago. After completing her studies at Elmira, she had spent a year in Paris, but even living abroad had not given her satisfaction. Still searching as much now as that day in the New England woods, Barbara thought of herself as a butterfly—fluttering from one interest or pursuit to another.

School was unfulfilling; so was teaching. Now she had come to Chicago to work with the George McGovern for President campaign. Even this was to leave her feeling empty and confused.

Barbara left Chicago with vague ideas of what to do next. The idealism she had hoped to satisfy in working for McGovern was still unrealized. Barbara reasoned, *Perhaps it's because I haven't personally sacrificed enough.* So she applied and was accepted for a job in the Peace Corps and flew to Togo, French West Africa, for her training. But before she made a commitment to continue Peace Corps training, Barbara suddenly became very uneasy.

I've got to get hold of myself, she thought. *I don't even know why I'm over here in Africa. This drifting and aimless wandering from one thing to the next is ridiculous! I haven't even taken the time to think about what I want to do professionally.* True, she had tried teaching. That had not given her satisfaction. Nor had her political involvement; and so far the Peace Corps wasn't filling the void either.

It's unfair to go on in the Peace Corps if I don't really mean business, she thought. Finally, Barbara decided to go back to the United States and try for a "last time" to pull herself together.

Back in America, Barbara had time to think about her future. At first she took a job in New York as a secretary. Then a girl friend told her, "You ought to get into acting school or become a model. With your good looks, figure, and voice, you can act rings around most of the people in acting school."

"Why not?" Barbara replied. "I've tried everything else, why not acting?"

ᗡᗡᗡᗡᗡᗡᗡᗡᗡᗡᗡ

Joe Colaizzi did not remember trying to kill himself. He woke up, looked at the clock, and saw it was almost time to leave for the university and his duties there.

Before leaving, his attention was drawn to the poster of Christ on the wall. He remembered pieces of a dream—or was it real?—in which he was calling upon this Christ for help.

"It was real . . . and I meant what I said," Joe said aloud. "If You're real—help me." He left the apartment for the university.

Joe parked his car and was walking across the campus when he heard someone call his name. "Hey, Joe!"

"Darlene . . . how are you?" he asked.

"I've been sort of getting myself together, Joe," she answered.

"I thought psychology majors always had their heads straight," he said, smiling.

"Well, this is one who didn't. But now I do, Joe. I went with Michael and Dick to this Jesus Rally two weeks ago and got saved."

"You got what? Jeez, Darlene, you sound like one of those Jesus freaks down on the mall," Joe laughed.

He looked at the young woman closely. There was something different about Darlene. Her eyes, once hard, now had a softness and clearness. Her face seemed more radiant, less puffy and tense.

"Joe, I just wanted to tell you, you don't need drugs to get high. Jesus gives me something better."

Jesus. A mental image of his wall poster flashed into his mind. *Help!*

"I thought of you right away. Joe, Jesus wants to help you, too," she told him.

"I . . . uh . . . I'm doing just fine," he said.

Darlene knew better, just as he did. She ignored his remark. "Joe, why don't you come over this evening. Michael, Dick, and I will pray for you."

"Pray for me?" he asked. Then he shrugged, "Okay . . . what have I got to lose?"

The others were already there when he arrived. Michael was a big man, a black whose deep voice reverberated with an unusual warmth and love. Dick was someone he knew slightly, but whose handshake communicated friendship and concern.

The first moments were spent sharing from their recent experience.

"Joe, you know how we always joked about people who 'got saved'?" Darlene asked.

Joe nodded.

"Well, we've all experienced a powerful and exciting transformation in our lives," Michael added. "It was something very *real.* We invited Jesus Christ into our lives—and by that I mean into our minds, our bodies, our souls, or whatever it is that makes us persons. And He *saved* us," Michael added.

Joe listened as each of them recounted what it was like. Though there were similarities, still each one had an individual experience with Christ to relate. Then they asked about his feelings, frustrations, and problems. They asked about his needs and how he thought God might be able to help him.

"Okay, I gotta tell you. I'm not a believer. I don't know what happened to you, or even if it did. But the way I feel now, I'll try anything. What's the first step?"

"You must admit you're a sinner, confess your sins to God, and ask His forgiveness. Repent—that is, agree to give up your sins and live by God's standards as He enables you," Darlene explained.

"Okay, then what?"

Dick answered him with a broad smile. "That's the best part. You simply pray to receive Christ into your life."

"That's it? That's all? How do I know it works?"

"Look at us. It has worked for us."

The two men came over to Joe and placed their hands on his shoulders.

"Let's pray," Michael said.

They all prayed, each building on the intensity and authority of the other's words. Through it all Joe kept his eyes closed and wished he could believe in this power.

Then Joe prayed, his words often jumbled and his mind groping for what to say. In spite of his inarticulate prayer, his spirit reached out in tentative faith. When it was over, he wasn't sure anything had taken place. Had God heard? Had something taken place? He had no feelings or sensations that indicated an experience had indeed happened to him.

But as he left, the outside world *was* somehow different. It was as if he had been transplanted into a universe where all the physical properties were the same, but the people, faces, and influences were changed. He sensed no oppression, no fear, no inner evil torment. Something *had* happened.

When he got home, he began to pray, think, and plan. He found a Bible and began to read it during the next week.

～～～～～～～～～～～～～～

Charlie Rizzo and his wife, Kathy, were packing for their move to Norwalk, Connecticut. Charlie had come a long way since that night when Paul Moore had searched him out at the high school and invited him to a unique new church. Charlie, an integral part of the New Milford revival, had been used to reach other young people for Christ.

Paul had tutored him for four years and Charlie felt ready to take on greater responsibilities. But his heart was deeply committed to New Milford. There were friendships and ties that were very precious. He wanted to stay and work in the ministry there, but he knew it was time to leave.

"You've been my shepherd and leader," he told Paul, "and I love you dearly as a pastor and a friend. But now I need to get out on my own. I have to show people that I can live and work outside your shadow."

The church held a big farewell party for Charlie and Kathy. Their departure was a loving, tearful time as the young couple left to become involved in a Connecticut church where Charlie would intern as associate pastor.

Ten

THE CONGREGATION IN New Milford, which had grown in numbers and confidence, had not been aware of Paul and Sharon's call to Manhattan at first. As it was revealed, there was a mixture of sadness as well as enthusiasm.

Longtime members (those in the church for more than a few months) preferred Paul's preaching and Bible teaching and generally felt comfortable with his leadership. However, there were some who had come to feel discontented and anxious for a pastoral change now that they knew Paul's heart had developed a new affection. Some of the congregation felt Charlie Rizzo should be called to come back and take Paul's place. However, both Paul and Reverend White believed that Charlie was not yet ready to assume such a responsible position.

Paul remembered a pastor friend from Michigan who had visited the Maranatha Church along with a number of his young people. On another occasion, he had stayed for a week to study the coffee house ministry and revival. The minister seemed genuinely interested and had the abilities required to be a replacement for Paul. He was a mature pastor who was also sensitive to the style, methods, and unique nature of the New Milford congregation. Indeed, Paul could not think of another person more suitable for the church's leadership.

Paul recommended his choice to Reverend White, who gave the minister a call. Before long, the man agreed to come.

From the beginning, Paul had begun training his converts to share their faith. The New Milford church regularly sponsored concerts and rallies where young people, especially, could hear about Jesus Christ. So it was natural for the church to encourage Paul by cooperating in outreach activities in New York to prepare for his upcoming move. Sometimes he took several musicians and their instruments and set up a sound system near a public park or college campus. Others would come along to hand out literature or talk with bystanders. Paul would preach, and nearly every such excursion would result in people coming to Christ.

✐✐✐✐✐✐✐✐✐✐✐✐✐

Bob DiQuattro was returning after lunch to his job as Postmaster at Columbia University's Teacher College, a job he had held for a number of years now since his return to New York when he had tried unsuccessfully to win back his wife.

He hardly thought of her these days. They had been separated for some time, and he had all but given up hope of a reconciliation. To take his mind off her and off the Fellowship, Bob had stopped going to church altogether and had started dating other women.

Crossing the campus mall, Bob was attracted by the sounds of a voice coming over a loudspeaker. Student radicals, speakers for gay rights, religious groups, and all kinds of people regularly used this forum. Usually he ignored them all, but this time he turned to listen. There was something familiar about the speaker.

As he walked closer, Bob saw a man about his age with thick, long hair, denim jeans, black boots, and a clerical collar.

I think I know that guy, Bob said to himself.

He stopped to listen as the preacher finished speaking. One or two young people stood near the platform chatting with several of the New Milford Christians. Bob edged closer.

"Paul Moore?" he asked. "Is that you?"

"Bob? What are you doing here? I almost didn't recognize you."

"And I nearly didn't know you. What are *you* doing here with these hippies?" Bob grinned.

The two friends embraced and brought each other up to date. They had not seen one another since working together a few years earlier with the King's Key Notes. Paul did not know Bob and Esther had separated, and he wondered how his friend was doing spiritually. "How are things with you and the Lord?" he asked with a smile.

His friend shrugged. "Okay . . . I . . . uh . . . haven't found a good church yet, though."

Paul asked, "Where are you living?"

"Clifton, over in Jersey. I live with my brother, Jimmy, and his wife."

"That's not far from us," Paul explained. He told him about Maranatha Church and its unusual ministry.

"Why don't you come and visit us Sunday?" Paul asked.

"Sure, I'll be there," Bob agreed.

His former habits were hard to break, but Joe Colaizzi continued to pray and think. He shifted from one plan to another, still confused. His mind was unstable. Finally, he called out to God one night, "Lord, I can't make even a simple decision. I think I ought to take some time off and learn more about this new thing. But where will I go? And who will teach me? God, *You* tell me where to go . . . when to go . . . and, so that I'll know it's from You"—Joe placed an "impossible" condition on his request—"somehow tell me through Dolly."

Colaizzi hadn't seen his ex-wife in several years. That she would get in touch with him was absolutely impossible, and Joe wished he hadn't made such a silly request.

Tired, frustrated, and confused, Joe began to weep and pray at the same time. "God . . . I'm still searching. I don't know what's happened to me or if I have anything at all. I don't know where to turn."

There was a knock at his apartment door. He got up and quickly went to answer. He opened the door and felt his stomach contract and hair stand out on his neck.

"Dolly!"

"Hello, Joe C.," she smiled, using the old nickname that had distinguished him from her brother, also named Joe. "Aren't you going to ask me in?"

"Uh, sure. Come on in. Sorry," he stammered.

"I don't know exactly why I've come, Joe C.," Dolly began. "But I was thinking that you probably need a vacation. I'll bet you haven't taken one in two years. Why don't you take off—get away for a while? Why don't you go to Sante Fe and visit my friend, Annie?"

Joe was almost shaking. Not five minutes earlier he had asked God for this absolutely impossible request. But even before he had asked, God was preparing Dolly to come! Somehow, for reasons of His own, God had heard him and honored his prayer.

 Eleven

IN THE EARLY autumn of 1972, Paul and Sharon scheduled a time for personal retreat. In addition to escaping the tension and stress of urban living, the two planned to spend time in prayer and fasting.

A Christian friend had offered them the use of his Long Beach Island summer home. Long Beach Island is a narrow strip of sand dunes, luxury cottages, and summer homes on an island fifteen miles long and a mile wide off the New Jersey coast.

By late September the tourists and vacation crowds were

gone. Only a few people remained. It was a perfect time and place to get away.

There was an enormous feeling of peace surrounding Paul and Sharon after just a few days of rest and relaxation. Hand in hand, they walked for miles together along the lonely beaches. Sea gulls soared and called out in their soft-harsh way. The cool air and overcast gray skies made everything seem fresh and clear.

Paul and Sharon prayed for New Milford, asking God's guidance for the church and its new leadership. They also prayed for money to launch a new church in New York, and for a place to meet there.

"Honey, I'm still really frightened about moving to New York City," Sharon admitted. "All of my 'motherly' instincts tell me it's wrong. Please pray that God will give me the peace of heart I need for this move."

Paul began to sense being released by God from his New Milford obligations. Everything was in place for a transition, at least as far as his replacement was concerned. Now it was up to God to care for the other needs: for the money, for a place to worship and live, and for Sharon's fears.

There was another personal element of this week of retreat that made it more meaningful than any other time together since their honeymoon.

It was Sharon's "fertile" week. As Paul and Sharon prayed, they asked for another child—this time, hopefully, a boy.

Paul told Sharon how his mother explained the story of her own prayers in a similar situation. His parents had had two girls—his sisters, Esther and Miriam—and likewise had prayed for a son.

"Even after she was expecting a child," Paul recalled, "she told me how she prayed and put her hands on her stomach, asking God to keep His hands on her boy. She just had faith that it was a boy."

Now, with their own two girls, Paul and Sharon prayed before their lovemaking that Sharon would become pregnant—and that it would be a boy.

Their Long Beach Island vacation was a beautiful time. Paul

and Sharon left at week's end rested, trusting God, and anxious to move ahead with His plan for their lives.

As they got in the car to leave, Paul impulsively shouted toward the clear skies, "Thank You, God, for giving us this wonderful time and place . . ."

". . . and for our *son,*" Sharon added, with a twinkle in her eye.

Twelve

BARBARA BILLINGS WAS accepted at the famous Lee Strasberg acting school. She had worked in New York City as a secretary for several months after her unsuccessful Peace Corps experience. But the hours of her drama classes overlapped with her schedule at the office. Barbara had to find another job where her hours could be more flexible.

She found just the right job as a waitress at Mr. Lee's Restaurant in Manhattan. It was a great place to work. Mr. Lee was a kind and patient businessman who had built his restaurant on the basis of fine food and service. It had charm and class. Barbara was grateful for a job so close to her apartment and studies . . . and at a place where she could feel comfortable.

Many aspiring actresses were forced to take jobs in less desirable places than Mr. Lee's. Some worked at small supper clubs as cocktail waitresses. Others worked in topless bars and danced to the noisy sound of a jukebox.

Barbara would never have considered demeaning herself in order to study and pay the bills. She would have to work in a respectable place and would refuse to give in to the pressures of big city life. There was so much sin around, though, that after a while it almost became commonplace, and to some was no longer shocking. Yet, Barbara knew she would never come to the place where she would compromise herself in order to achieve success.

One evening after work, Barbara hurried along the darkened street to her apartment. Usually she walked with a friend for safety, but tonight she had worked a bit later than usual and had missed that opportunity. She pressed her purse tightly to her side, and as she walked she watched for anything suspicious. She sighed with relief as she unlocked the vestibule of her apartment building and went inside. She picked up the mail from the box in the lobby and pressed the elevator button.

Barbara sorted through the bills and circulars and noticed a letter from her brother, a senior at Wesleyan University. Robert wrote:

Dear Barbara,

It was good to hear from you and see you over the holidays. Nice to hear about your job and acting classes, also. It was interesting to read in your letter about your dissatisfaction with your life and the problems in finding meaning and purpose. I guess I didn't really relate to that search until this year at the university. But lately I've been asking the same questions that you wrote about. You might be interested to hear that at last I think I've found the answer in Christianity. A group of Christians on campus calling themselves "InterVarsity Christian Fellowship" have been helping me find the answers in the Bible and Jesus Christ. I think the answer to loneliness and finding personal fulfillment is found in Jesus Christ, and in knowing God through Him personally. Please don't go to the fortune-teller your friend Cari told you about. Wait until we can get together and I can explain.

Barbara was intrigued after reading the letter from her brother. She didn't understand what he was referring to but was interested in its possible answers. She would follow up the matter with him sometime.

Joe Colaizzi did not leave immediately for Sante Fe to visit Dolly's friend. It took him a week to finally decide that God indeed was working in his life.

A week later he withdrew two hundred dollars in cash from

his account and took off for New Mexico. Joe wasted no time on
the road. He pulled over periodically for food, gas, or a nap; but
essentially he drove straight through—a distance of nearly two
thousand miles in three days.

Annie was a little surprised to see the unexpected stranger,
but she greeted him warmly. "Why are you in Santa Fe?"

Joe shook his head. "I don't know . . . yet." He explained what
had happened to him.

"Far out," Annie said. "*God* told you? Far out." A supernatural
explanation was entirely plausible to her. She regularly con-
sulted horoscopes and occult charts for advice.

A few days later, after feeling rested and more relaxed than
he had in years, Joe asked Annie out to a local pub for
dinner.

As Joe and Annie sat in the booth, a young man walked over to
them.

"Excuse me—mind if I dance with your date?" he asked.

"No . . . go ahead," Joe replied.

Annie nodded and the two of them walked to the dance floor.
While they were gone, Joe prayed.

"Lord . . . I don't know why I'm here in Sante Fe. I know I'm
supposed to be here. But I only have a little money left. If you
want me to stay, You'll have to give me a place to stay."

Annie and her dancing partner came back to the booth. He
introduced himself and sat down.

"Annie told me you came down from Pittsburgh. Gonna stay
long?" he asked.

"I dunno. I'm not sure."

"Well, listen, Joe. If you need a place to stay while you're in
town, I've got plenty of room. You're welcome to move in with
me."

"I can't believe it," Colaizzi told them. "I can't believe what I'm
hearing!" He didn't explain but accepted the man's offer.

Joe spent the next few days reading his Bible and thinking.
Everything was falling into place, except *why* God had brought
him to Santa Fe.

Later Joe went to a shopping center with his new roommate
who wanted to look at some Indian jewelry at a silversmith shop.

Joe waited outside in the mall area, reading his Bible to pass the time.

Once again Joe thought of his dwindling resources. Even though he had a place to stay, he still had to eat and buy other necessities.

"God, I don't know why You brought me here yet, but I believe You will tell me when You're ready. But if You want me to stay in Sante Fe, I will need a job. I've got fifty dollars—only enough for gas back to Pittsburgh, so I would need to leave right away. I don't have any idea where to look for a job."

Joe had just finished his prayer when a Spanish-American man came up to him and said in broken English, "Mister . . . are you looking for work? You can get a job there at the restaurant." He pointed across the mall. "The cook goes on his honeymoon and they need part-time dishwasher. You want?"

Bob DiQuattro and another friend, Wayne Rogers, came to dinner with Paul and Sharon and listened to the cassette tape Paul had made months earlier when he had driven through Manhattan. Both were moved, and they volunteered to help establish the work in New York.

"Okay," Paul said, "but first I want you guys to drive over to Manhattan. Like Joshua's two spies, I want you to go up and down the streets near East Sixty-second and visit the clubs and singles bars. Come back with a report on whether or not there is a mission field there, and if there is, be thinking of a strategy for witnessing and sharing Christ to the people in those bars."

Wayne and Bob drove to Manhattan the next night, armed with Scripture pamphlets and a cassette player to record their impressions.

They made this report.

> We visited several clubs and found various receptions. Some bars were noisy. It's difficult to witness with loud music or dancing in the background. It's too distracting. But all in all, we're very encouraged. In fact, in one instance, while we were canvassing the clubs and singles bars, we went into one place and Wayne met a waitress from his old high school. We witnessed to her and, after

she got off work, introduced her to Wayne's girlfriend. After more sharing and prayer, the girl accepted Christ as her Savior and expects to come to our church as soon as it's established!

Thirteen

PAUL WAS IN Pasadena to address a workshop for the Los Angeles District Church Schools Convention for his denomination. The convention wanted to hear about a project he and the New Milford church were running for neighborhood kids who weren't enrolled in a Sunday school.

"We started a whole network of sandlot or backyard Sunday school classes," Paul told them. "We taught them Bible lessons and won many of them to Christ. In order to attract the kids, some of us went to New York where the Children's Television Workshop has its headquarters. They gave us a tour of the *Sesame Street* production and explained how the Muppets work. We went back and created our own authentic replicas of Big Bird, Oscar the Grouch, Kermit, and the rest of the gang. Well, it drove the kids wild. Word of mouth advertising packed out all the backyard classes. Our biggest problem was in keeping the parents away!"

His workshop was held at the First Church of the Nazarene in Pasadena. Many people of the church, including its respected pastor, Dr. Earl Lee, had heard of Paul through the denominational publications. The New Milford Church of the Nazarene had been featured on numerous occasions for its unusual methods but outstanding results in evangelism.

Hazel Lee, the pastor's wife, heard Paul share something of his burden for the people of New York and told her husband, "Earl, you need to talk with this young man!" So later, Dr. and

Mrs. Lee had dinner with Paul and asked him to explain his ideas.

For nearly an hour Paul sketched his dream for a church in the middle of Manhattan—a Nazarene church—where one was so desperately needed.

Paul's voice began to build in excitement; and he got louder as he continued. "The Church of the Nazarene simply *has* to share in the burden of Manhattan and its one and a half million people. The city has more Jews than Tel Aviv, more Germans than Hamburg, more Blacks than Swaziland. You know, we have seventy missionaries in Swaziland; that's one missionary for every six thousand people. If we were that concerned for Manhattan, we would have 262 missionaries there! We don't even have *one*. Even Maine has fifty-three Nazarene churches, but Manhattan doesn't have one. Not one!" Paul pushed his dessert plate away and paused to sip his coffee.

Dr. Lee reflected as the young man talked of his dream and calling. His mind went back over thirty years to when as a young couple, he and Hazel had tried to make a dent on that great metropolitan area from a church in Flushing. *But we hardly raised any dust during those fourteen months in New York,* Dr. Lee thought. However, he and Hazel had never lost their love and concern for that area.

"How much money do you need to be the first?" Dr. Lee asked Paul.

Paul thought quickly. "Well, we plan to raise maybe $15,000 from the church we're starting . . . the twelve people who will come with me from New Milford can help me talk the denomination into donating $5,000 or $10,000. But I'll need another $30,000."

"You've got it," Dr. Lee said quickly.

"Wh-what?" Paul stammered.

"Our church will put you on our missionary budget. Come back in April and share your story with our people. We'll help you."

Paul knew the time had come. He called Reverend White and said excitedly, "If you have my replacement, I've got the money! I'm coming home in order to go to New York!"

Reverend White rejoiced with him. "That's terrific news. Praise God! I sort of thought the Lord would work this way. I've written five thousand dollars into my budget for your work in New York, Paul. And I have a commitment from the Department of Home Missions at headquarters in Kansas City for another $15,000."

"That's frosting on the cake," Paul said gratefully. "It's almost as if the Lord gave us that as a bonus. It really confirms our calling. Now, all we need is a place to worship. Thank you, Brother White."

Fourteen

PAUL BEGAN TO take periodic trips to New York City to hunt for a meeting place. He thought of several older churches already in the midtown area whose congregations had dwindled. He planned to ask for permission to rent one of these buildings at times when it wasn't being used for services of the existing church.

One day he came across an old and beautiful structure that was a landmark on East Sixty-first Street. He noted from the sign in front that the building housed a Baptist congregation. Paul looked for a way to get inside, but the church was locked. A parsonage or caretaker's apartment was on the side and he went back to ring the doorbell.

An attractive, slim woman (Paul guessed her to be about forty) answered the door. She noticed his clerical collar and smiled warmly.

"Good afternoon, Reverend. May I help you?" she asked in English, but with a decidedly Scandanavian accent. Paul noticed that she then seemed a bit taken back by his jeans and boots.

"Good afternoon, Ma'am. I'm Reverend Paul Moore . . . and I'm starting a new church in Manhattan. We're people who love the Lord, and we're looking for a place to meet on Sunday afternoons for worship and some week night for Bible study. I'm wondering if your church would rent us the use of the building when you're not using it?"

"Come in, Reverend Moore," the woman said extending her hand. "I'm Martha Stenstrom. My husband is the sexton and chairman of our church. I'm sure he would be most happy to discuss this with you. Won't you have some coffee and cookies—he should be home any minute."

Over coffee, Martha explained, "Our church has been without a pastor for a long time. Many people have moved away. We have a minister named Walter Martin who is teaching a Bible study."

"I know Walter; he's a good man," Paul commented.

"Since our pastor resigned, we have not had a regular minister."

Paul was aware of the flight from established inner city churches not only of pastors but also of their congregations. The two largest evangelical churches in New York City had recently received resignations of their well-known ministers and had not yet found replacements. It was typical of what was happening.

"We have been praying for a long time that God would find a way to use the church. Dr. Martin teaches a Monday night Bible class . . . and on Sunday morning about twenty-five people come to church. That's all," she recalled sadly. Then her eyes sparkled, "You should come to our church board and make a proposal!"

Her husband, Edsel, concurred with his wife's idea when the three of them discussed it later. Edsel earned his living as a builder. He was a skilled carpenter who had used his gift to repair and remodel the church and parsonage. The church had been built originally in 1930 (at a cost, then, of $650,000) by Swedish Baptist immigrants and their descendants. It had beautiful stained glass windows and a hand-crafted decor throughout. Edsel's fourteen years of care showed in nearly every area of the mammoth building as he had nearly single-handedly worked to fix, replace, polish, or renovate.

Edsel's Swedish accent was as quaint and charming as his

wife's. Their hospitality was genuine, and they worked with Paul to make an appointment with the board.

The evening for the meeting came and twenty-nine members of the church were present, along with Edsel and Martha. Edsel, as chairman of the church, presided. Paul was late, and so Edsel explained to the church members some of the general ideas of Paul's plan.

Martha stood and told the members, "We have prayed many times that God would revive our work here. I think Reverend Moore is the answer to our prayers. The church will bring in young people from the East Side and at last will be used in a real way."

A preliminary vote was taken before Paul arrived: It was a tie with several abstentions. Edsel wished Paul were there to present his dream of a growing new church, an outreach to the younger generation.

Nearly an hour after the meeting had begun, Paul showed up. Innocently, he had gotten the time confused and therefore was late. However, a few on the church board seemed irritated by his tardiness.

Then, more than a few were upset when Paul strode to the front to speak. Several of the older members were so put off by his clothes and long hair that they did not even hear his words.

They were not impressed with their youthful guest or his friends who had come along to sing and play. The old people feared the noise would wear out their building!

A second vote was taken. Some of those who had voted against the plan claimed they had additional "no" votes from out-of-town members. "We have their proxies," one woman said.

"But that's not parliamentary procedure," Edsel told them.

There were brief arguments, and the meeting ended without a vote. Edsel, trying to keep things peaceful, suggested the church postpone their decision and call a second special meeting to decide.

By the time of the second meeting, those opposing Paul and his group had encouraged out-of-town members to be there in person. The general superintendent from the Baptist offices in Chicago was also on hand. A stormy session followed as the general superintendent reminded the people of their heritage and the need to preserve that heritage.

"Are we more interested in heritage than saving souls?" Edsel asked him.

"I'm interested in seeing that this church preserves its heritage," he answered.

"Look," Edsel explained, "We're not asking them to be involved in our worship services. Reverend Moore only wants to rent our facilities when we're not using them. They want to meet on Sunday afternoon and Friday night. And you know that the rent could help ease our financial problems."

There was more discussion as Edsel and Martha looked at each other sadly. Edsel looked around the room and counted fourteen votes of people who had wanted the new church. He mentally added up fifteen votes—including those people who hadn't been to church in months or years—of those who opposed Paul.

Edsel stood to speak. His voice was ready to break as he announced, "I can see that there are more ready to vote against than for. I am heartbroken to hear that our church is more concerned about heritage than salvation! I cannot stand by and risk God's judgment at such sinful behavior! If you vote this way, I am afraid you will bring God's judgment down upon your heads! I know my family cannot worship here and feel at home any longer. We have talked it over, and after prayerful thought I am submitting my resignation."

It was a deep blow. After fourteen years of such emotional and spiritual ties, Edsel and Martha were cut loose. As sexton, chairman, and guiding force behind the church, he, along with his wife, had struggled (more than anyone knew) to keep the church on a positive financial basis.

At home that night—their action completed and their resignation final—Martha and Edsel wept bitterly.

Fifteen

AN EASTER SUNRISE service at Cooper's Pond in the spring of 1973 was the final one for Paul and Sharon at New Milford. More than one thousand converts, friends, and clergy came to celebrate their risen Lord and say goodbye to the Moores. It was a beautiful and meaningful service of farewell, as the Moores were commissioned for their work in New York.

With a "going away" banquet hosted by the New Milford congregation, the $20,000 committed from the denomination, and the $30,000 pledged from Pasadena, Paul left New Milford with Sharon (her pregnancy now obvious to all) and the children for New York City. Twelve "Daresaints*"—six single adults and three couples—were to follow them from the New Milford congregation to help get the church in Manhattan off the ground. These loyal friends had demonstrated their concern for evangelism and their willingness to commit their time, money, and energy to make the experiment work. They were also experienced "witnessers" who would be able to share Christ in the singles clubs of Manhattan.

Because of the high cost of real estate in the city, Paul suggested they look for a place where, initially, several of them could live and the church could hold services. They found a four-story building on East Seventy-second Street, which they rented for $1,500 a month. On the first floor was a kitchen, dining room, and large entrance. Doors there opened onto a spacious back porch and garden with a lovely southern expo-

---

*A Daresaint is defined by Paul Moore as one willing to attempt great things for God regardless of risks; the opposite of a daredevil.

sure. During the warm months, services could be held outdoors in the garden.

On the second floor was a large living room and study. Sharon and Paul would live on the third floor with their children. On the top floor, rooms were set aside for the three single girls and one unmarried man. The others in the group found apartments with each other in the Upper East Side area.

The place was ideal not only for its housing and facilities for worship services and Bible studies, but also for its strategic location. It was close to the kind of people who would respond to Christ, grow in faith, reproduce themselves, and make a church in Manhattan financially viable.

Their target group was the affluent, upward-striving, single young adult and career couple twenty-two to thirty-five years old. Wayne Rogers, whom Paul had been discipling for a year, and Bob DiQuattro worked with Paul on the demographics of their target area—the Upper East Side. Building on their original observations as "spies" earlier in the year, they developed a working file on every singles bar in the area, including such information as who the bartender was, what kind of music was played (live or jukebox), what their hours were, and whether or not they featured dancing. They developed their own literature and witnessing tools. For example, instead of using the "Four Laws" tracts, they memorized the material and sketched diagrams of the four principles with felt tip pens on cocktail napkins. The approach seemed more natural and less "canned."

By the end of April, everything was ready. On Saturday, May 1, 1973, they would move into the town house and hold their first church service the next day.

II. New York, New York

Sixteen

LOADING THE U-Haul truck for the move into Manhattan did not seem like work for the missionary "Daresaints." It was a time for supercharged enthusiasm and excitement.

The truck was loaded by late Friday night, and on Saturday morning, the clear skies seemed to show God's blessing on the move. As they crossed the George Washington Bridge, tall buildings seemed to cry out with their need. "Some twenty-six *million* people live within a seventy-five mile radius of this spot," remarked Paul as the big truck rumbled along.

The entourage of the truck and two cars split at the bridge, the truck making its way down Broadway and the cars speeding their way on the West Side Highway to hasten their arrival. Each of the passengers seemed gripped with the daring adventure they had begun, alternating noisy conversation with silent reflection.

The U-Haul and cars pulled up in front of the four-story town house on Seventy-second Street. It was an answer to Sharon's prayers that they had been able to find a nice home in a clean and relatively safe neighborhood.

After a full day of unloading and carrying in cartons and furniture, the men and women were fatigued and sore. Muscles ached from countless trips up and down the fifty-one steps of the staircase. Finally, subdued and silent, they sat in a circle in the living room, holding hands and conversing in quiet prayer with the Lord.

They were all pleased, grateful, and expectant—sharing a sense of common destiny after their first full day in the new parsonage in Manhattan.

As the group was moving into Manhattan, Bob DiQuattro prepared to act.

Try as he might, Bob was unable to get Esther out of his mind. Although neither had specifically filed for a divorce, they were for all practical purposes already divorced. Bob had not seen Esther in nearly two years.

There was no voiced criticism of this from the New Milford church or the group going to New York, although many questioned his situation. Many of these new converts and renewed Christians were from strict fundamentalist church backgrounds. They had earlier rebelled against what they felt was a legalism in the church, often identifying more readily with the counter-culture.

There were similar incidents in the New Milford church that would not have occurred in a more mature evangelical church, especially regarding the use of alcohol, tobacco, and the choice of entertainment. The transition from the former sinful lifestyle, with its excessive drinking, drug use, and sexual promiscuity, in all too many instances was not quick and decisive. In an attempt to be tolerant and relate to the youthful counter-culture and lifestyle, the church sometimes exercised poor self-discipline in matters of separation from the ways of the world.

Bob had earlier felt justified in dating other women, especially when he had been away from the church and out of fellowship with Christ. Now more than ever, however, he wanted a reconciliation with Esther.

"But I can't ever see that happening," his brother Jimmy said. "That cult group has such control over her, she'd never even listen to you."

"I know," Bob replied sadly. "But . . ."

"Yeah?"

"I've been doing some thinking—what if we got her away from the group. When we first got married and lived in Pennsylvania, she seemed all right. It wasn't until she left for New York that she got messed up again. I think if I could get her away and talk sense to her. . . ."

"You'll need help," Jimmy responded.

"I know. I think I'll call that guy I read about in *Time*—he's an expert at deprogramming people who are brainwashed by cults."

The next day Bob called Ted Patrick who offered to help if Bob would pay his expenses. Within a few days Patrick and the two brothers were driving in Esther's neighborhood, monitoring her schedule, following her to meetings at the prophetess' Fellowship. They made notes of her routine and planned an abduction for Saturday, May 1—the same day Paul and Sharon were to move into the New York town house.

The three men rose early that morning. Bob was the most nervous of the trio. It was decided that Jimmy would drive the car. Ted Patrick and Bob would hustle Esther into the waiting vehicle—without force if possible.

"There she is!" Bob whispered hoarsely. Esther was walking briskly along Broadway on her way to a meeting. Bob opened the car door before Jimmy had stopped and leaped onto the sidewalk behind her. Hearing the running footsteps, Esther stopped and turned. Recognizing her estranged husband, she froze momentarily, not knowing what was happening.

"Esther, I want you to come with me!" Bob shouted. Esther panicked and tried to run. Bob seized her and wrestled with her. Esther screamed and kicked in her attempt to free herself. It took both men to force her into the back seat of the car. Passersby heard Esther's calls for help, but they weren't sure how to respond. The car doors slammed, and the vehicle screeched off down Broadway.

"Esther, please, stop screaming!" Bob yelled. His wife was hysterical. "Please, we aren't going to hurt you! We just want to talk."

It was several moments before she was able to calm down. "What are you doing? Where are you taking me?" she cried.

Ted Patrick answered, "We're going to a motel to talk. Your husband loves you very much, Esther, and he wants to talk to you about getting back together."

"I think instead of going to a motel as we planned we should go to Pennsylvania to my folks' house," Bob said.

Patrick shook his head. "That's no good. If the authorities become involved after that scene back there, that's the first place they'd look. Let's stick with the plan and go to the motel."

"No!" Bob was adamant. "Look, I've already upset her more than I had planned. I don't want to terrorize her. She'll feel more at home at my folks' place. Besides, they'll cover for us if anyone asks."

In a few hours they were at the home of the DiQuattro parents. After an explanation was made to Bob and Jimmy's mother and father, Ted Patrick asked Bob to spend some time rebuilding a good relationship with Esther. "She's afraid and needs some comforting," he said.

Patrick had previously briefed Jimmy and Bob about what to expect. The plan was to first let Bob reassure Esther that he and the others meant no harm. It was to be made clear that it was because of Bob's love and concern that he had resorted to these desperate tactics. Hopefully, when Esther came to believe this and relaxed, it would be easier for Patrick to perform the actual "deprogramming."

Bob and Esther started to talk, but their every word revealed tension and hostility. Esther was still crying, and it looked as if it would be a long time before the mood changed.

The awkward scene was suddenly interrupted by a loud pounding at the door. "Ted Patrick and DiQuattro, this is the police! We have a warrant for your arrest on federal kidnapping, conspiracy, and assault charges. We command you to surrender immediately!"

Bob's father opened the door slightly and tried to tell the officer outside that he and his wife were alone in the house. The cop responded by ripping the storm door off the hinges and forcing himself inside. He was followed by several other officers, all with drawn guns. Quickly they forced Jimmy and Ted Patrick against a wall and frisked them, then roughly handcuffed their hands behind their backs. Bob had no time to react before the police rushed into the room where he and Esther were. Esther began to shriek once again.

"It's okay, lady. We're the police and FBI."

"What's going on here?" demanded Bob. "This woman is my *wife.*"

"Are your Robert DiQuattro?"

"Yeah."

"And are you Esther DiQuattro?"

Esther nodded, still sobbing loudly.

The policeman continued, "We have a warrant for your arrest. Esther's mother has filed kidnapping charges against you three—and crossing the Pennsylvania line makes it a federal charge."

"But she's my *wife*! I love her," Bob implored.

"That's some way to prove it, buddy." Then he turned to Esther. "Are you here of your own free will? Do you want to be with this man, Mrs. DiQuattro?"

Esther seemed brought down by the whole episode. She began to cry uncontrollably. "No! I've been kidnapped! They brought me here. I want to go back. I want to be with my mother!"

"That's enough for me. Read 'em their rights and book 'em!" the cop declared. Then he turned to Esther and said kindly, "Get your things and we'll see that you get back to New York."

Paul and Sharon had nearly collapsed from fatigue after moving to the New York town house on East Seventy-second Street that Saturday. It was well after midnight before they got to bed and fell asleep. In the morning they would have the first worship service in their new setting.

Paul was tired and fell asleep immediately, but Sharon had some difficulty relaxing enough to sleep. Her tired aching, body was especially sensitive to a chore like moving. Just three weeks before the anticipated birth of their third child, Sharon had insisted on helping clean and scrub floors before the others moved around the furniture and boxes. Finally both were sleeping soundly.

It was early morning when the telephone roused them.

"Hello? Bob . . . what's the matter? You're *where*?"

After a hurried telephone conversation, Paul was unsure of the details; but he tried to explain what he knew while dressing.

"It was Bob DiQuattro. He's in the Tombs, the city prison, on federal charges of kidnapping, conspiracy, and unlawful imprisonment. The FBI arrested him and Jimmy after following them across two state lines! It has something to do with Esther. They extradited him to New York. I've got to go see him and find out what's happened."

Then as an afterthought Paul added, "This isn't exactly the way I had planned our first day here!"

The sensational aspects of the incident made front page news and television headlines. Most people, including the authorities, seemed sympathetic to Bob. Yet, in truth, he had broken the law.

Paul spent considerable time in prayer with Bob and Jimmy, assuring them of his support and availability to help in any way.

"The case goes before a grand jury to see if I'm to be indicted and held over for trial," Bob told Paul. "And things don't look good. We probably would have been released but we hear the assistant district attorney wants to get at Ted Patrick. In order to get him to trial, they have to indict us all."

Paul said, "Well, God knows your heart in this. Your actions were done out of loving motives. I'm sure He'll understand that. Just trust Him in this whole situation. Put some faith in Romans 8:28, Bob. This will work out for your good. You'll see."

In spite of more sensationalizing by the press and aggressive legal maneuvering by the D.A.'s office, the grand jury refused to indict Bob and the others. The assistant D.A. appealed, but the grand jury refused to reconsider. The case was dismissed and Bob, Jimmy, and Ted Patrick were released.

Meanwhile, Bob learned that Esther was no longer in New York. She had gone to South America, apparently afraid of being kidnapped again. Through fragments of information from different sources, Bob learned that the Fellowship, led by the prophetess, had moved their operation to Cali, Colombia. Bob sent Esther letters, but they were either returned unopened or went unanswered. It was as if she no longer existed.

Seventeen

BOB AND JIMMY DiQuattro felt even closer to the new Manhattan Church now. The love and community its people had shown them during their ordeal convinced Bob that God was at work in the life of this new effort. Without marital responsibilities, he was able to spend long hours witnessing and working for the new church. Soon he lost himself in a multitude of church duties, hoping to take his mind off Esther.

Shortly after the opening of the Manhattan Church of the Nazarene, a new music group was formed. It took its name from a parallel someone made between the first Manhattan Project (code name for the discovery of the atomic bomb) and the church's new outreach for New York City, dubbed the Second Manhattan Project. The music group called "The Manhattan Project" consisted of Bob and Jimmy DiQuattro, Sharon Moore, and newcomer Judi Cochran.

Judi was single and able to spend more time with the charter development of the church. She had raised her support from her home church in California and came to serve as the church's first full-time staff member.

Judi was an accomplished soloist whose beautiful clear voice added rich musical depth and charm to the singing group. Her blend with Sharon and the men was superb. They sounded as if they had been singing together for years.

However, Judi had other responsibilities as well. Her job was to disciple the women in the group of twelve who had come with Paul and Sharon to help start the church.

Effie Jansen, the converted night club entertainer, was one of those who also came to help with the church. Manhattan was Effie's home, and so she was glad to worship and serve in a place so near. As a new Christian she began to study the Bible and grow in her spiritual experiences. Effie was not at all intimidated by the thought of going out witnessing with the group, in spite of the fact that they often returned to the clubs and bars where she had entertained. She had lost none of her uniqueness or sophistication, and her testimonies were always quite effective.

Sharon found she had little time to be frightened over the move to New York City. Her life, busy before, was now hectic in a most fulfilling sense. She began to have more of a role with Paul in the outreach of the church, especially when opportunities for singing were present. As "house mother" at the town house, Sharon was the one who was often up all night—not only with her own children when they were sick but also with the young people living with them when they were sick or suffering bouts of loneliness or homesickness.

Three weeks after they moved into the East Seventy-second Street town house, it was time for another interruption.

It was four A.M. and Sharon sat upright in bed.

"Paul, I think my contractions have started," she said. Paul called Wayne Rogers who borrowed a fifteen-year-old battered VW bug for the trip back over to New Jersey. Sharon's doctor was in Bergen County and on staff at Holy Name Hospital.

On the way, Sharon grew anxious. The borrowed car gasped and groaned—sputtering as if it wouldn't make the trip. Sharon tried not to think of the VW breaking down. Instead she tried to focus on giving birth and the joy that comes afterward. As she reflected, however, she shuddered, *for Cathi had been born with a rare blood type and complications had developed.* Consciously Sharon turned her cares over to God and tried to relax. Soon they would be at Holy Name Hospital.

As Paul paced the waiting room floor, waiting for news from the delivery room, he covenanted again with God to give his offspring wholly to the Lord. Both he and Sharon took seriously their responsibility to "raise up a child in the way he should go." Their family devotion times, both as children and now as parents, were among their most highly treasured memories.

Their prayers were answered. The baby was born healthy. And Sharon's faith was also rewarded. Their third child came to live in the parsonage, the newest occupant of the East Seventy-second Street town house. And it was a *son*—Paul Sartell Moore II.

 # Eighteen

BY SUMMER, 1973, the Manhattan Church of the Nazarene was the talk of the denomination. When Paul had presented the challenge to the people of Dr. Earl Lee's church in Pasadena in April, the $30,000 needed to start the work was raised in just six minutes.

The people pledged not only their dollars but also their prayer support; eventually ten summer-intern missionaries travelled from California to New York. A prayer network for the Second Manhattan Project was established. Tape cassettes of Paul's impassioned April presentation were sent to out-of-town members and college students. One of them was Michael Christensen, a student at Eastern Nazarene College in Boston. He listened to the tapes and quickly became enthused. "At last," he told one of his dorm buddies, "our church is doing something about social concerns as well as evangelism. This New York thing sounds like something I could really get excited about." Mike did not even go home following the end of the school year. He packed his gear and went directly from Boston to New York as the first missionary intern for the Manhattan Church.

The witnessing in bars and singles clubs continued to be the primary outreach of the fledgling church.

Years before Paul took the New Milford church, he had spent a brief stint as a part-owner of a singles bar at Ninetieth Street and Second Avenue, and worked three or four nights a week as a bartender.

Paul winced as he remembered that regrettable time—at the hours he spent "evangelizing people to sin," instead of helping them know the Savior.

However, as he reflected now he took heart, knowing that God will even redeem past prodigal experiences. God worked *all* things for good, for who else was better equipped to witness in the singles bars and clubs? This was Paul's old "turf." He knew the area and it's people. He had looked into their lonely faces and listened to their hurts. Unlike when he had been behind the bar, he had some answers for them.

The technique of sharing the Christian faith in bars had been thoroughly tested and refined by now. Those witnessing ordered club sodas with a twist of lime so they had a "drink" while listening to someone. Only after listening for a half hour or more to someone did they feel they had earned the right to talk. Even then, they chose their approach carefully. Using the "felt-tip pen sketch on cocktail napkin" idea, they shared in a natural way how Jesus Christ loves people and relates to their needs. The teams learned that it was best not to approach a couple— they were there to be with each other and resented "intruders." Nor did they distract from the real issue by having a guy witness to a girl or vice versa. Usually the best approach was two guys talking to another guy, or girls talking to girls.

The witnessing was quite effective. The initial twelve disciples brought in that same number of new disciples during the first few weeks. The converts came to worship on Sundays and to Friday night Bible studies where they became grounded in their understanding of the Scriptures. By July, forty or fifty people were regularly showing up for the Sunday brunch and worship service.

SHEPHERD OF TIMES SQUARE

One of those who witnessed regularly was Jim Hullinger. Jim had a Nazarene church background and had attended Olivet College in Illinois. He had known all the right answers so far as fundamentalist Christianity was concerned, but as a young adult he had strayed from the church and its influence. The temptation to conform to the lifestyle of sin in the big city had captured him long enough for bad habits to be firmly established.

However, at age thirty-two, Jim received Jesus Christ as his Savior and determined to rebuild his life and habits. Not too long after his conversion, Jim had gone to the New Milford church and told Paul he was praying for him to begin a work in New York. Now, almost a year later, Paul was there. Jim showed up on May 2, the first day of services in Manhattan. Somehow he had learned of the move. From that day he was committed to the ministry. He worked part time at the L'Marquis Hotel and devoted almost all of his other free time to the church. Jim was involved in the planning of the new church's programs and projects from the beginning. He put in long hours, often matching Paul's own rigorous schedule.

Martha and Edsel Stenstrom were also among the first visitors on May 2. When the pain and grief of leaving their once-beloved Trinity Church subsided, they decided to join in worship at the Manhattan Church of the Nazarene. Despite being middle aged, they were among the more "youthful" worshippers to become charter members of the congregation when the church was officially organized.

Almost prophetically, three months after the awful night of Edsel's resignation, a series of sobering events befell the old church. The vice-chairman who had strongly opposed the plan and had spoken out against Edsel, died of a heart attack; another vocal couple watched their daughter lose her mind and saw her committed to a mental asylum; another couple failed to keep their home when the husband lost his job of many years; and the church, as it was, fell apart.

Paul's strategy for building a church in Manhattan started with winning people to Christ from the affluent Upper East Side from Sixtieth to Eighty-sixth streets, east of Lexington. He hoped to capture the interest and allegiance of the career couple or sophisticated single—the "Bloomingdale's" crowd. By starting with a core of financially stable members, the church could become self-supporting and go after those less able to financially support a church ministry—such as vagrants, prostitutes, and addicts.

As they brainstormed creative and effective ways to reach the apparently inaccessible affluent high-rise dwellers, several ideas were considered.

The most attractive for its simplicity, economy, and visibility was "The Balloon Project."

A prestigious high-rise apartment building was selected as their initial objective. Someone suggested a way to communicate with these dwellers that at first seemed silly. But as they thought it through, it had real appeal.

"There are 2,580 windows in that building," Paul told his volunteers. "Now imagine what would happen when the harried Manhattanite comes home from work, goes into his apartment on the seventeenth floor, and by 6:15 pours himself a martini and looks out the window. Just outside is a balloon with a message, 'Smile, Jesus loves You. Call 988-7420.' We'll have a hundred or so people down below on the street holding onto the string and letting the balloons go up, floor by floor, on all four sides of the building. Can you imagine the residual effect that'll have with the TV news people? Let's do it!"

Paul felt that Nazarene friends across the country were watching him. He thought he had to justify to Dr. Lee's church, Reverend White, and others what they were doing in New York with their funds.

This strategy would give them visibility as a church, to say nothing of the advertising value of the balloons.

However, as the day grew nearer for the event, Paul had second thoughts. During Bible reading, he read Proverbs 19:21.

"A man's heart may be full of schemes, but the Lord's purpose will prevail." God seemed to be directing Paul to abandon the balloon idea.

Paul was deeply touched by the Scripture—as if God Himself were saying to them, "I am more concerned with relationships than activity; *being* comes before doing. Do you think twelve people—or a hundred for that matter—can do My purposes without My help? Can you outrun the cabs? Can you outshine the lights of Broadway? This work is too big to be done in your own strength. Your 'schemes' won't work."

Paul called a moratorium on everything that smacked of "action." He immediately cancelled the balloon project and called his extended family around him to teach six principles of "being comes before doing."

ONE: BEING COMES BEFORE DOING—We must slow down and wait for God to act and prepare the way. God doesn't want us to be "super activists," trying to justify our existence by how much we *do*. And just as we do not want God to love us for what we do—but rather for who we are—so God wants us to love Him for who *He* is not for what He does. This kind of living lets God set the pace for us.

> Commit your life to the LORD; trust in him and he will act. . .
> Wait quietly for the LORD, be patient till he comes; do not strive to outdo the successful. . . (Ps. 37:5,7).

TWO: MINISTER UNTO THE LORD—We must become practicing priests, offering up each part of our being as a living sacrifice to God. Our thoughts, our emotions, our speech, our "acts" must all be turned Godward to bless His heart.

> Therefore, my brothers, I implore you by God's mercy to offer your very selves to him; a living sacrifice, dedicated and fit for his acceptance, the worship offered by mind and heart (Rom. 12:1).

THREE: BE SUBJECT TO AUTHORITY—We must establish a spiritual chain of command for our lives. God is a God of order and requires us to submit ourselves to each other for the sake of Christ. God cannot accomplish any significant work on earth or release His individual and collective blessing until His people follow their leadership.

> Obey your leaders and defer to them; for they are tireless in their concern for you, as men who must render an account (Heb. 13:17).

FOUR: BE WASHED BY THE WORD—We need a daily scrubbing of our minds with God's Holy Word. The purified, renewed mind is a must if anyone wants "to know what is good, acceptable and perfect—the will of God." God-inspired ideas and knowledge of the holy will come only to the persons who think God's thoughts, feel God's emotions, know God's plans.

> And now, my friends, all that is true, all that is noble, all that is just and pure, all that is laudable and gracious, whatever is excellent and admirable—fill all your thoughts with these things (Phil. 4:8).

FIVE: LET THE HOLY SPIRIT DREAM IN YOU—We must let the Holy Spirit dream a new dream in us each day. Then our lives will be unique, authentic, personal—and thus effective. *He* will lend His mind-expanding influence and enhance the powers of imagination and creativity beyond our expectations.

> Adapt yourselves no longer to the pattern of this present world but let your minds be remade and your whole nature thus transformed . . . (Rom. 12:2).

SIX: BE A DARESAINT—We are now ready to realize our spirit-inspired dreams.

> Things beyond our seeing, things beyond our hearing, things beyond our imagining, all prepared by God for those who love him (1 Cor. 2:9).

Nineteen

JOE COLAIZZI FELT that the physical effects of drug and alcohol abuse were behind him. No longer did he awake in the middle of the night, sweating, screaming, and scared. Perhaps the clean New Mexico air and consistently sunny climate also contributed to his inner healing. Yet, that was only part of the reason God had brought Joe to Santa Fe.

The owner of the restaurant where Joe applied for work as a dishwasher was a well-to-do businessman in the community. As it turned out, he owned not only the restaurant but also the entire shopping center—including a Christian book store in the center of the mall. Joe saw at once the reason for his being there. Christians worked beside him at the restaurant; he had a job and place to stay; and he had believers who took a personal interest in his well-being. They demonstrated their love for him and helped him begin the patient rebuilding of his lifestyle, philosophies, and habits.

Over the next seven months, Colaizzi began to mature. His employer provided books and studies for him to nurture his new faith, and Joe grew stronger in Christ.

He all but forgot about Dolly, about Pittsburgh, about his former life. So enthusiastic was he about his new "being" that the months went by quickly. Yet Joe knew he couldn't stay in Santa Fe, working as a dishwasher-busboy forever. Some time he would have to move on. But he resolved to use the same mystical approach to the decision that brought him to Christ in the first place—trusting God for specific guidance. Even in the small areas, Joe had learned by now the habit of relying upon God for answers and direction. As his mind had cleared over the months, his thoughts and prayer life had become more articulate. He now sensed that perhaps it would soon be time for the next step of God's plan for his life and whatever new experiences that might involve.

ᴼᵛᴼᵛᴼᵛᴼᵛ ᴼᵛᴼᵛᴼᵛᴼᵛ ᴼᵛᴼᵛᴼᵛᴼᵛ

Barbara Billings seemed to be drawn to the letters her brother wrote from the university. "I have come to believe in Jesus Christ as a result of the InterVarsity program here on campus," he wrote her, "and I'm praying that you'll come to know Him, too. The experience has opened my mind to so many new things and provided answers to the questions and problems we've talked about in the past. I hope you'll think about coming to Christ."

Barbara wasn't all all certain what her brother meant by "coming to Christ" or "knowing Him." She had heard the words before, but the phrases seemed part of an "inside" language that the more religious young people on campus had used. Words such as "saved," "coming to Christ," "throne of grace," and others she'd heard but couldn't remember meant absolutely nothing to her. Perhaps if someone defined or interpreted them they would make sense, but just now she didn't understand.

Barbara decided to visit her brother and talk with him about his own experience. She took the bus to the campus of Wesleyan University and found him. He was happy about her visit and invited some Christian friends over. Barbara at first felt uneasy talking about religion in such a casual setting, but these young people soon made her relaxed.

For nearly two hours they talked about Jesus. Each friend told about his background and conversion experience. That's what believers called "witnessing" she learned.

"Just remember, Barbara," one of the guys told her, "God will never turn His back on you. If you sincerely seek to know Christ, He'll reveal Himself to you."

Her brother gave her a book to read on the trip back to the city. "It's a book to help you grow in the Christian faith if you make your decision." Still not sure what it was all about, she took the book and thanked them for their interest.

Later, while waiting for the New York bus, Barbara took out the book. She opened it hesitantly, not knowing whether it would make any sense to her.

She directed her thoughts toward God, wishing somehow He could grant her whatever it was that her brother and his friends had.

Barbara opened the book and read the introduction.

This book will have little meaning for you unless you know the Lord Jesus Christ personally. If you do not know Him, here is a prayer for you to receive Him.

She continued reading. "You are a sinner." Yes, she understood what that meant, especially after hearing the Scripture references her brother's friends had read to her explaining that *"all* have sinned" by not living up to God's standards. "You have done wrong things to other people and especially to God," the book continued.

Yes, that's right, too, Barbara admitted to herself.

"Do you believe that Jesus Christ is the Son of God?" *Yes.*

"Do you want your sins to be forgiven?" *Yes, of course.*

"Then pray this prayer: Lord Jesus, the Bible teaches us that we come to God through You. I admit my sinful condition and nature. I am truly repentant and willing to have my life changed. By faith, I come to You, asking for forgiveness for my disobedience. I claim Your promise that You will forgive me and transform my life here on earth and prepare me for eternal life in Your presence, a place the Bible calls heaven. I pray for Your Holy Spirit to come and live within me so that I may be born again. Thank you, Lord, for doing this in my life. Amen."

As Barbara finished praying, a calm, reassuring presence swept over her. An inner peace and positive mental awareness confirmed the reality of the experience, and she knew instantly that conversion had taken place.

Twenty-year-old Michael Christensen was attracted originally by Paul's shirt-sleeve approach to starting a church. Mike's

minister, Dr. Earl Lee, could have used a talented and committed young person like Mike in his own church, but he willingly
sent Mike and other volunteers to help launch the Manhattan
Church. Most were summer interns. A couple of them, it turned
out, would cave in from the pressures and stresses of New York
"culture shock."

Mike's first encounter with the realities of life in New York
City came quickly. The first week he was there he found a young
man—glassy-eyed and nearly unconscious from an overdose of
drugs. Mike tried to resuscitate him, but the teenager failed to
respond. Panicky, Mike spotted two policemen and called them
over. "This boy needs an ambulance!" he told them. The officers
shrugged and dragged the boy out of the gutter to a nearby
alley—out of traffic—gave him a kick or two to try to wake him.
When that didn't work, they shrugged again and walked away,
leaving Mike staring in unbelief.

Mike and the remaining volunteers "hung in" for the summer
and helped the new church by sharing Christ in Upper East Side
singles clubs or the parks.

At summer's end Michael was so overwhelmed by the love of
the New York church group and the results he saw from his
witnessing that he decided to stay on for the next school year.

"But what about college?" Paul asked him.

"I'll take a year off. I'm just so caught up in what's happening
here that I can't leave just now. Besides, a year here will give me a
more mature context from which to decide about long range
goals and career choices. I've talked it over with my parents and
Dr. Lee, and the idea has their blessing. I want to help you start
this church!" he stated emphatically.

Barbara Billings didn't say anything to her co-workers at Mr.
Lee's about her new-found faith in Jesus Christ. Nor did she
speak about it to any of her classmates at Strasberg's acting
school. She did phone her brother to tell him what had happened to her, and he was delighted.

However, some of the earlier excitement and the feelings at

conversion were now only memories, feelings that Barbara could not conjure up upon demand. The experience was definitely real, in spite of the growing time-span since that day when she prayed to receive Christ. Some of her former doubts and frustrations returned to nag her, so Barbara sought advice from her brother. He encouraged her to do two things: "You need to study the Bible and get into Christian fellowship with other believers. You need to find a good church."

Barbara wondered how to find such a place to worship. She prayed. "Lord, help me find a church that will help me grow."

Twenty

IN MID-JUNE, SIX weeks after the arrival in Manhattan of Paul, Sharon, and the other disciples from New Milford, a telephone call came to Paul from Joel Tucciarone.

"Reverend Moore, I'm not sure you know me. I saw you last fall on the David Susskind TV Show and at a Jesus Concert at Carnegie Hall. We met recently at Jerry Davis's church."

"Yes, Joel, I remember. What can I do for you?"

"I'm a Christian in advertising. I've been asked to work on the "Key '73" evangelistic project for New York by editing the Key '73 newspaper. But that's not why I'm calling."

"How can I help, Joel?"

"Well, I just got a call from Frank Baker at the American Bible Society. They were to sponsor a "Key '73" concert in Bryant Park."

Paul recalled that Bryant Park was located behind the public library in midtown Manhattan, just a block from Times Square. It was a perfect location for a Jesus concert. Paul listened as Joel continued, "Everything has been done. We have the park permits, police and park personnel ready to help out, a terrific PA and sound system. We have ten thousand copies of Scripture portions to hand out and everything. There's just one problem."

"What's that?" Paul asked.

"Our musical program fell through" Joel answered. "What can you suggest?"

Paul thought only for a few seconds, then he had a full blown plan for Joel. "This whole thing may be ordained by God," he said. "Our group has been preparing for six weeks for something like this. I believe we're ready spiritually and musically for your concert. We can handle the whole thing—music, testimonies, handing out Scriptures, counselling inquirers, everything."

"That's super!" Joel answered and shared with Paul the details of what had been done so far to prepare for the Bryant Park event. Paul knew now that his "being before doing" principles were correct. *God* had prepared everything for them to step in.

A few weeks later most of the church body and intern volunteers turned out for the Bryant Park "Day Spring '73" Jesus concert. Jim Hullinger set up a literature table and other Christians, mobilized by both Paul and the Bible society, began to distribute thousands of *Good News* booklets. Others pumped helium into hundreds of balloons (left over from the scrapped balloon project) that proclaimed "Jesus Loves You" and listed a phone number for more information.

The concert consisted of performances by the Manhattan Project, Effie Jansen, folk guitarist Gail Swain, and several other rock or folk-music groups.

Paul spoke briefly between musical sets and urged listeners to respond to the call of Jesus Christ for salvation, forgiveness, and new life.

The "Day Spring '73" concert became an eight-hour-long event. A number of people responded to Paul's brief sermons and prayed with church members to receive Jesus Christ.

Many more people approached the group to ask serious questions about the music, the comments of performers, or Paul's messages. Some even wanted to know what church was putting on the event.

One young woman had been pedalling her bicycle up Sixth Avenue to the park. She carried a kite and her Bible for an afternoon combination of relaxation and study. As she got to Bryant Park, she heard rock music with lyrics about Jesus Christ coming from the sound system. A crowd had gathered to listen to the "Jesus Freaks" sing and play.

Getting off her bike, the young woman wheeled it toward the edge of the crowd. *Is this some weird cult,* she wondered, *or are they really Christians?* As she listened to the sermon, the content seemed consistent with what she believed.

A college-age man handed her a balloon and literature. "Hi," he smiled, "My name is Peter Pasqualino from Manhattan Church of the Nazarene. I'd like to invite you to our worship services on Sunday."

The young woman smiled, "Your church sounds exactly like what I want. My name is Barbara Billings . . . and I'll see you on Sunday, Peter!"

 Twenty-one

THE BRYANT PARK "Day Spring '73" concert was the first of eight concerts produced for Bryant and Central Parks that summer by the Manhattan Church.

Paul learned that the parks were available without charge for such purposes. All one needed was a permit, readily available from the park department. In fact, not only could the church use the parks without charge for its concerts, the city of New York even helped. The park department employees would set up benches for two thousand people and the police department would provide its assistance.

The successful concerts and witnessing in the singles clubs caused the church to grow significantly over the summer.

By Labor Day, Paul was preaching to an average Sunday crowd of eighty to one hundred people; and forty-four people—many singles—applied for charter membership into the new church. It was a truly heterogeneous group, including Dave and Nancy Stuckey, the Stenstroms, Jim Hullinger, Bob DiQuattro, and Effie from nearby; Bea Grushow, Judi, Wayne, and others from New Milford; Barbara Billings and many new converts from the concerts; a few couples and many singles. A variety of racial, social, economic, and ethnic backgrounds were represented. There were models, advertising executives, actresses, secretaries, an airline stewardess, an artist, and others from all parts of Manhattan whose lives had been transformed. They gathered on Labor Day for a most unusual event—to celebrate something that had really already taken place—the birth of Manhattan Church of the Nazarene. This meeting officially chartered its membership.

The church met this day in its new facilities. After being turned down by Edsel and Martha's former church, Paul had looked around for another church with a willingness to rent space for Sunday afternoons and one weekday evening.

He finally discovered Immanuel Lutheran Church where the congregation could worship temporarily.

There were more than two hundred people at the gothic Lutheran church for the service on Labor Day to organize the church and charter its first members. For many of them, it was their first church experience. These had been converts for a month or less: *Todd,* who made a profession of faith that day; *Chittu,* converted through street preaching; and *Lisa,* disillusioned former disciple of Maharajah Ji and a new Christian.

Reverend Jack White, from the Nazarene district headquarters, officiated, and Raymond Hurn, executive director of the denomination's department of home missions, preached at the service.

Paul Moore was officially installed as minister and participated in the service of Communion that marked the acceptance into membership of the forty-four new applicants.

What had begun as a small group a little more than three

months earlier was now an active congregation. Every Sunday night their new church was a growing reality—a phenomenal answer to the prayers of many people in many places.

Twenty-two

ONLY A FEW months after the church was officially organized, Paul was shocked by a call from a fellow pastor across town.

"Paul, I have terrible news. Jack White has died."

The words struck Paul deeply, and he felt his stomach turn. He hung up the telephone after receiving the news and stared into space.

His mind went back to their first meeting, years ago at New Milford, when Paul had asked for the chance to start a church work there. Jack had come into a service in the middle of a rock concert and wasn't sure what these young people had in mind for the church.

Once again Jack's words after that first meeting came to Paul. "Everything in my being says I should pull you out of here and toss those kids and their awful music out of this church! That sound is loud and terrible, and everything you're doing here goes against everything I believe and feel. But I *can't*. For some reason, God is working here. He's doing something very real. I don't understand it, but I'm going to let you stay."

The silver-haired patriarch from district headquarters had been Paul's friend. When questions or complaints came in from other churches or pastors about Paul's methods or style, they had been routinely funneled through Jack White. He had blunted many of the hard criticisms that came from honest misunderstandings. Through it all, Jack White had understood

Paul Moore. It had been good to have an understanding friend on the "inside" at headquarters.

Paul sat by the phone for several sad moments as his thoughts went to the fifty-eight-year-old, white-haired conservative church leader. Paul quietly thanked God for Jack White, and knew he would be missed. He wondered, also, about future relations between himself and the denomination. Now, with Jack White gone, it would be even more important to rely on the mature counsel of Chuck Blake, George Gressett, and Ken Huber. These three district lay leaders were serving as an initial church board for the youthful Manhattan Church that had not yet developed that kind of leadership.

Several days later Paul was one of the pallbearers at Brother White's graveside services. He grieved for his friend and wished he had not been taken so soon.

∽∾∽∾∽∾∽∾∽∾∽∾∽

With summer gone, Paul wondered about a new outreach to the community to replace the concerts in the park. The small church began to pray for new avenues of witness.

Part of that prayer was answered one evening when Paul and Sharon were at home relaxing. Paul went over to check the *TV Guide*. "Not much good on tonight," he said, adding, "I wonder what's on cable TV."

Cable TV offered a few more choices than just the New York City broadcast stations. As licensee for CATV in half of Manhattan, Manhattan Cable was obligated to provide "public access" opportunities in addition to the entertainment and sports shows they imported. "Public access" meant that any individual or group could go before the cameras on a TV channel specifically designated for public programming.

The results were often unintentionally funny or entertaining as many of the city's resident "kooks" exploited this chance for instant notoriety.

Since there were no restrictions, viewers were given a cross section of the city's interest groups: Spokespersons for Gay Pride, Lesbians for Liberty, and a dozen other similar organizations and a few quasi-organized groups were given free time.

However, public access meant that religious groups could have an equal footing on the channel with some of the homosexual or counter-culture groups.

Paul discussed with Dave Stuckey his ideas of TV concepts. David had his own television camera and videotaping equipment. He offered the equipment and his own leadership to start a television outreach. John Hillyer, an NBC-TV cameraman, offered his experience and skills as well.

Paul called on the church to pray about a possible television ministry on cable TV. The church members thought it was a great idea. Before long the Manhattan Church of the Nazarene had purchased a camera and TV recording equipment and was producing thirty hours of television a week. They became the largest producer of public access programs, featuring taped replays of the Sunday worship services, Wednesday night Bible studies, musical programs, debates, interviews, sermons, and the like.

ᴗᴑᴗᴑᴗᴑᴗᴑᴗᴑᴗᴑᴗᴑᴗᴑᴗ

Continuing to look for a permanent church location, Paul was excited when he learned of a possible solution one day.

"Listen to this," David Stuckey said to Paul as he read from *The New York Times*. "They're trying to auction off an old Staten Island ferry that they've taken out of commission. It has three decks and two thousand seats. No one has bid on it, and they think it'll be sold for $5,000 scrap. Why don't we buy it? We can find a berth on the East River . . ."

"And renovate it. We could remodel it a deck at a time," Paul jumped in, seeing the possibilities.

"It could have an auditorium, restaurant, and theater on the first deck . . . a chapel on the second deck . . . parsonage on the third deck," Paul dreamed.

The two men brainstormed the concept of acquiring the ferry for a church home. They could berth the ship near public transportation and public parking.

For two months they pursued the idea, but in the end it proved unworkable. There was only one berth available, too far from public access to be practical. Besides, although they probably could have acquired the ferry for $5,000, cost estimates to refurbish it were prohibitive and Paul abandoned the idea.

The new church continued to grow. Before long the basement quarters at the Lutheran church were too cramped and the Manhattan Church was forced to look for yet another home, its third in less than six months.

Paul discovered another church willing to let them rent space. It was the old Swedish United Methodist Church located on Sixty-second Street near Lexington, a fashionable town house neighborhood.

The pastor, the Rev. Ronald Law and his wife, Madelyn, agreed to share their church with the congregation and their folk music instruments, although some of the church's older members weren't as enthusiastic. The pastor told Paul, "Of course, we'd be happy to have you worship here. We have an eight o'clock service on Sunday morning, and an Estonian group meets here Sunday at one. But you can use the building after three o'clock and on Wednesday night."

Twenty-three

BARBARA BILLINGS WAS happier than she had ever been in her life. She still worked at Mr. Lee's and was showing great spiritual maturity and growth.

No longer afraid to speak to others about her faith in Christ, Barbara began by telling her co-workers about Him. Cheryl Cooper was the first to hear. Cheryl had only begun working at Mr. Lee's recently after some "sleazy" waitress jobs elsewhere. She had come to New York from Oklahoma to study at The

American Academy of Dramatic Arts. She had applied for work at the restaurant during the summer break and was hired.

Cheryl had always thought of herself as a Christian. She'd gone to church regularly back in northwest Oklahoma. And in college, she had been sympathetic to a Campus Crusade representative who shared Christ with her. As she thought about it, though, Cheryl could see her ideas of Christianity and God were different from Barbara's.

"Why don't you come to church with me on Sunday?" Barbara asked Cheryl. "Our pastor is *so* with it! He's young and has contemporary ideas—and doesn't put people down. You'd like him," she added.

"Maybe one of these days," Cheryl replied. "I have to work this Sunday, though."

"I'll trade with you so you can go," offered Barbara.

"No . . . that's okay. I don't want to go by myself."

"You could go with Larry," suggested Barbara.

"Uh . . . no . . . sometime later, maybe."

Cheryl was living with Larry. That was one way Cheryl's "Christianity" differed from Barbara's. Cheryl knew that Barbara's faith was different. Perhaps it was this dynamic young minster of hers. She thought about Larry again. Even from her limited church background, Cheryl knew it was wrong for her to be living with Larry. It was "normal" behavior for aspiring young actors and actresses, but somehow she sensed it was wrong.

◌◌◌◌◌◌◌◌◌◌◌◌◌◌

As more and more people began to come to the Manhattan Church, its people became more conscious of their successes. Paul's preaching continued to be positive and evangelistic. Hardly a week went by without several people receiving Christ and joining the church.

Paul rose early in the morning and was at the office long before anyone else. He studied and wrote his sermons, counselled people, taught them, and directed their evangelistic activities—often until well past midnight. Seldom did he take time off. When he did interrupt his routine, it was generally to work on an article for the denominational magazine or to speak at a ministerial gathering.

In spite of his hectic schedule, Paul jealously guarded the hours on Tuesday nights after dinner. It was time that he devoted exclusively to his family. The youngsters knew they could enjoy Daddy and not have to compete with church members for his attention. Paul was aware that even if there were eight days in a week, he would still have a hectic schedule. That's why he worked hard to protect this "family night," one evening a week when he was exclusively theirs.

If Sharon had any complaints about Paul's schedule it was that he needed to have a "wife night" in addition to "family night." As there were more and more demands on her husband's time, she saw him less and less. She caught herself many times feeling jealous of other women in the church who saw more of him than she did.

Their holidays were also crowded. At Thanksgiving, Christmas, and other holidays, Paul invited the lonely people without families to have dinner with him and his family. It was rare for Sharon to cook for fewer than twenty people at holidays.

Sharon and Paul seldom had time alone, in spite of the fact that Paul set aside some time for Sharon in his schedule. Even in bed at night their prayers or lovemaking were often interrupted by a telephone call from someone in need.

Sharon knew her husband loved her. He often told her. Lately, however, she had wondered if his love might not be more from a sense of duty than from attraction. Sharon was often ill at ease around other women, yet she didn't know exactly why. Sometimes, she felt threatened by "ravishing" career women her age who had not borne children and still had their teenage figures and dress size. The birth of each of her three children, Sharon noticed, had exacted some loss of muscle tone, added stretch marks, and widened her hips.

While undergoing this transformation from girl to woman,

Sharon had never thought of the change in positive terms. She often wished Paul would tell her how gorgeous she looked instead of saying the obligatory "I love you."

All these factors seemed to overwhelm Sharon and her feelings about herself. The situation was further complicated by her frustration over the difficulties of being a mother in New York City. She and Paul did not own an automobile, and so the youngsters had to be walked to school for safety purposes. Music lessons, doctor and dental appointments, shopping, and the usual weekly round of duties were always difficult and sometimes scarey trips by subway or bus.

Frequently her day would end in tears and fatigue. Complaining to Paul brought no real satisfaction. His idea of dealing with her problems was to give Sharon an "encouraging" talk, to try to lift her spirits by playing down the seriousness of the problem.

"Look, all you need to do is get a hold on yourself and your emotions. *All* wives have things rough, but they aren't impossible. You can do it if you (and here the answer varied slightly)

> —only get a grip on yourself."
> —only get organized."
> —only pray about it."
> —only get up an hour earlier."
> —only put a little more effort into it."
> —only go to bed an hour earlier."

Increasingly Sharon resented this simplistic approach and felt Paul really knew nothing at all about her life and needs.

Twenty-four

PAUL HAD IMPORTANT dreams for his new church. However, before these were launched, he decided to prepare the church spiritually for growth.

"Let's have an old-fashioned revival meeting," he suggested to several key leaders. "It'd be very 'hip' in New York. We could bring in branches of trees with autumn leaves, scatter sawdust in the aisles, and decorate the place like an old-fashioned church."

The others picked up on the idea. "Yeah, we can use lanterns and candles."

". . . and an old pump organ for music," suggested someone else. "And I found some one-hundred-year-old hymnals in a box here in the church basement."

Paul invited an old friend, Reverend Ron Pelton, an excellent preacher and evangelist, to come and present the gospel message. The staff produced a brochure to distribute and posters to tack up that invited people to "an old-fashioned revival meeting. You'll hear music and sermons from the past. Dress in your best calico and overalls and come with your friends!"

This slightly theatrical approach would interest many in Manhattan, Paul knew. "They won't know whether it's a show or for real—until they come out."

As the date drew nearer, posters all over the East Side told about the event. People in the church, themselves new converts for the most part, did not know quite what to expect.

Barbara Billings told Cheryl Cooper at Mr. Lee's, "It'll really be different and exciting. I've never been to a revival meeting."

"I have," Cheryl said softly. "Years ago in Oklahoma. I don't suppose they have many in New England where you're from. But down home, we have them all the time."

"Will you come then?" asked Barbara.

"I guess so," Cheryl answered.

The church basement was packed with curious people on the first night of the week-long series of meetings. Everything was in place, decorated just as planned. Also, as expected, the people were not sure at first that this was not a show. It took a while for them to understand that the service was "for real."

Ron Pelton's preaching left no doubt about that. He preached an old-fashioned gospel message but with plenty of twentieth-century application. Before he finished the sermon, many were weeping in genuine repentance.

Scores responded to Pelton's invitation to "come forward and be saved." Among them, sobbing and moved dramatically, was Cheryl Cooper. Her conversion was decidedly *real*.

Another who went forward in tears was Warren Campbell, a forty-five-year-old homosexual. He confessed to the preacher that he had become a Christian in a Nazarene church as a young man but had drifted far from God and was completely backslidden. He also knew that getting right with God meant turning his back on his gay lover, leaving the homosexual community and culture, and probably losing his job—since his work was also strongly tied to the gay lifestyle. Yet, as Warren confessed his sin and prayed for reconciliation with God, Paul saw that he meant business. Paul prayed with him and told him he would help Warren work himself out of the gay lifestyle.

The next night, the service drew another full house. One who went forward to receive Christ with many others was Cheryl's roommate, Larry.

They went home exhilarated and excited about the transformation in their lives. They talked about the experience for hours before going to bed. However, Cheryl and Larry suddenly became aware that sleeping together was wrong and were seized with conviction and guilt.

"We can't do this," Cheryl said tearfully. "What are we going to *do?* We can't go on sleeping together."

"I know," Larry replied. "I'm sorry . . . I just didn't think . . ."

"Neither of us thought much about it before. But we can't do it anymore, now that we both know it's wrong," Cheryl said.

"What should we do now?—I mean about sleeping together. It's three in the morning," Larry asked her.

Cheryl reached for the telephone.

"What are you doing?" Larry asked.

"I'm going to call Reverend Moore. He'll know what to do." She found the brochure with a phone number and dialed.

A sleepy voice answered on the other end. Cheryl, quickly explained their dilemma to Paul. He reassured them that God would understand it if they just turned over and went to sleep for now. Then in the morning the two of them could come into his office and they could discuss their circumstances.

The next day Paul advised the couple to break up housekeeping. He helped locate a Christian guy in the church as a roommate for Larry, someone to help him learn more about his new-found faith in Christ. Cheryl moved in with a spiritually strong Christian girl to be likewise discipled.

The revival services had a profound effect on dozens of people in the East Side community. Lives were dramatically transformed and entire families, social circles, and even businesses were forever changed.

Barbara Billings had been the only believer at Mr. Lee's. Now there were two. Barbara and Cheryl grew in their understanding and faith and began to share their lifestyle and beliefs with other co-workers.

Before long, Beverly Irving was the third contact. Beverly was a stunningly beautiful model—a "Clairol girl" and talent for many TV commercials and magazine ads—who worked at Mr. Lee's between jobs.

Three months later, Cari Brendel, a pretty girl studying to be an actress, gave up her tarot cards, Satan worship, and occult practices to become a Christian because of Barbara and Cheryl.

Todd Dexter, good-looking actor-busboy, was also won to Christ when the others shared their experiences with him.

During those first months a standard was established by the first converts; no one would leave employment at Mr. Lee's without seeing his or her Christian faith reproduced in someone else working there. It became a natural thing to win and disciple people so that there was someone to carry on the work of Christian evangelism when they left.

Twenty-five

I T WAS SHORTLY before five A.M. and Sharon woke instantly, thinking she heard a strange sound in the house. She listened carefully to see if it was one of the children getting up to go to the bathroom or for a drink of water.

She heard the noise again—heavy (not a child's) footsteps in the next room. Was it Paul? She felt next to her, both reassured and frightened.

"Paul!" Sharon whispered as loudly as she dared, shaking her husband. "Someone is in our house and coming down the hallway to our room!"

Paul rolled over, still asleep. She tugged at him frantically as she spied a man's shadow on the wall outside their bedroom. Immediately her mind recalled an instance just the week before when an intruder had shot and killed a young husband and brutally raped his wife while their helpless children were forced to watch. Sharon was terrified. "Paul! There's a man in here!"

Paul was now fully awake and his heart was racing. The intruder walked toward the bedroom, and Paul sat up in bed quickly. The two faced each other at the edge of the darkened room.

"What do you want?" demanded Paul. Sharon screamed. In an instant the man turned and ran. Only when they heard the front door slam did Paul and Sharon breathe easier.

Paul got up, turned on the lights, and checked to see if anyone else was still in the apartment. When he was certain they were safe, he called the police. Sharon was still shaking with terror when the police came and investigated the break-in—the intruder had broken a window to gain entry.

"He was probably a cheap crook looking for an easy score," one of the detectives told them. "I doubt if he had a weapon or he wouldn't have run. He probably thought you were away—this happens all the time."

Paul and Sharon had been burglarized twice when they were living in the East Seventy-second Street town house. Once the office had been robbed and the Sunday offering stolen while they were away. Another time, when they were on a church retreat, their home had been ransacked. The robber had broken the door and taken everything of worth, including some things that had mostly sentimental value. Missing also was Paul's coin collection, a prized treasure from his childhood that he and his dad had worked on together.

Although Paul changed all the locks and reinforced the windows, Sharon still slept lightly, jumping at every unusual night sound or rustle.

ひひひひひひひひひひひ

After seven months of spiritual growth in Santa Fe, Joe Colaizzi prayed for three weeks about what to do next. "Lord, I'd like to go back to Pittsburgh and work with Joe (his former brother-in-law) in his construction business. But he knows me only as the guy I was a year ago. He'd never ask me to come if he thought I was the same person as before. But how can I tell him I'm different? If You want this for me, and it's not just something *I* want, then *You* work it out."

Joe's prayers were uncomplicated and straight forward, like himself. They were also full of faith, a result of his having seen God work in his life previously.

Therefore, it came as no surprise to Joe to see his prayers answered. First, he received a telephone call from Dolly.

"Joe C., it's me! I'm in Albuquerque. Can you pick me up?"

"Of course. I'll come right away."

It took Joe just a little over an hour to drive sixty-two miles on Interstate 25. He found his former wife and greeted her warmly. During the trip back to Santa Fe and Annie's apartment, Dolly listened to Joe's exciting story of what had happened to him.

"I can tell *something* happened to you, Joe C.," she smiled. "You're a different person—softer, nicer."

They soon got to Annie's, and the friends had a brief reunion; Joe was asked to stay. They talked about many things, including Joe's changed life.

"Before it gets too late back East, I'd like to call home," Dolly told her. "I promised Mom and Dad I'd call when I got here."

After the usual pleasantries were exchanged, Dolly called Joe over to the phone. "It's Joe, my brother. He wants to talk to you."

"Joe C., hey, it's good to hear your voice. How long has it been . . . nearly a year? Yeah . . . say . . . Joe, I've got a proposition. We just bought an old farmhouse and want to remodel it—turn it into an apartment building. Uh, I was wondering . . . you're really good at that sort of thing. Do you suppose you'd ever consider coming back to Pittsburgh and working for me?"

Joe smiled broadly, his dark eyes shining.

"Sure, Joe. I'll be up there within a month. Soon as I clear things up here."

"Great, buddy. You can even stay with my brother, Ron, while you're here. It won't cost you anything for a room. We'll see you then."

In New Milford, Paul's former church was going through transitional complications. The congregation had called Charlie Rizzo back from Connecticut to be the associate pastor.

Shortly after he and his wife, Kathy, had arrived, Maranatha Church encountered difficulties. The minister who had agreed to come from Michigan to replace Paul was not comfortable in the role. He came to the conclusion that he was not equipped with Paul's intuitive understanding when it came to ministering to the congregation.

In simple terms, it was not working out. The pastor submitted his resignation and returned to Michigan. The Maranatha Church called Charlie Rizzo to be its new full-time shepherd.

Charlie had been growing in his relationship with the Lord, and now—like Paul—was pursuing his theological credentials through a rigorous self-study program, looking forward to the day he would be ordained.

Hope was nearly gone for Joyce. Since 1969 she had been a street prostitute working the Times Square area. Unlike the Upper East Side call girls who earned up to $1,000 a night, Joyce had to hustle for her money. That meant working the crummy bars, approaching men on the street, waving down cars—trying to get as many "johns" as she could since her pimp never gave her enough money.

She had tried holding back on him, but more than once he had savagely beat her. Now, Joyce had two problems that were occupational hazards: a severe case of gonorrhea and a $100-a-day heroin habit.

She had tried unsuccessfully to kick the drugs. Recently, she had even tried to detoxify her system from the addiction by going to a city Methodone clinic. But she had overdosed on that supposedly harmless drug and nearly died.

Now, Joyce was totally broken and had absolutely no desire to live. In fact, she wished that she *had* died from the overdose.

Her pimp had no regard for her when she was unable to hustle. And, certainly the men who bought her body didn't really care for her. Joyce hated those men—all men, really. She also hated herself for the degradation she let them impose on her body and spirit.

There was no one really left to turn to. Even her lesbian lover seemed to have little comfort for her now.

Joyce knew she needed help. She'd heard of the Walter Hoving Home for Girls and had scribbled its address on the back of a match book. The organization had something to do with God or religion. She was certain God must have already abandoned her, but decided she had no where else to turn.

Twenty-six

PAUL WAS HAVING a breakfast meeting with Wayne Rogers, David Stuckey, Jim Hullinger, and Mike Christensen. The five men sat somewhat cramped in a large booth in a coffee shop on East Thirty-ninth Street. As they ate and discussed church business, the streets began to crowd with commuters on their way to work.

"Do you recall what we learned last spring about waiting on God? About 'being before doing'? We prayed and waited for God to lead and open doors for us. We learned that God is already at work in circumstances and at the right time will involve us in His plan."

Paul pushed his plate away and motioned to the waitress for a coffee refill.

"What I'd really like to see is for us to build on that principle and stretch our faith with a second concept," Paul said. "I want our people to learn that there's a supernatural element to Christianity."

"Like the power of prayer?" Mike asked.

"Yeah . . . but more than that. You know, like the really great things God can do when we let His Holy Spirit dream through us. It's a reminder of that 'being before doing' commitment of allowing God to do the groundwork—to go before us and care for things. We can do more great things if we commit ourselves to that concept and let the Holy Spirit work.

"I've had some thoughts. It's helped me fashion what I call a 'daresaint theology.' And I get the concept from two verses in the Bible. The first is Romans 12:2 and the second is 1 Corinthians 2:16*.

"Man, what a thought! Let God the Holy Spirit dream through you, because, one, our minds have been transformed; and two, we have the mind of Christ already in us," Paul explained.

"What do you mean by 'the Holy Spirit dreaming dreams through us?" Mike asked.

Paul began to elaborate on the concept. "Unless a person has dreams and works to see them become reality, there's no chance for success. That's a 'success formula' that will work for anyone. He doesn't have to be a Christian. But with the mind of Christ in us with the Holy Spirit to challenge our imagination, we have a plus factor. Our dreams are in partnership with God. And He can open a lot more doors than we can on our own—*impossible* doors for us."

"So you think we ought to ask for some 'impossible' thing and try to pull it off?" Wayne asked.

"Yeah . . . exactly. Something that cannot be pulled off, humanly speaking. Something that would have to have God's hand in it in order to work."

Mike nodded. "I've talked to many of the new Christians, and I know God has worked miracles for them in their lives—people like Barbara Billings, Cheryl Cooper, Warren Campbell—nearly everyone, come to think of it, has a story like that."

"And it's exciting to hear about someone's success with the Lord. But I think our church needs something like that to unite us in corporate faith for even more fantastic things ahead," Paul told them. "Anyway, that's my idea—so let's pray about it."

*Romans 12:2—"Adapt yourselves no longer to the pattern of this present world, but let your minds be remade and your whole nature thus transformed. Then you will be able to discern the will of God, and to know what is good, acceptable, and perfect."

1 Corinthians 2:16—"For (in the words of Scripture) 'who knows the mind of the Lord? Who can advise him?' We, however, possess the mind of Christ."

Several days later, Paul found his "faith project."

While talking to a New York Council of Churches' representative, he learned that the man was responsible for public service time for radio and television in New York. Usually his job was to line up speakers for the sign-on or sign-off "sermonette." Sometimes he was asked to suggest articulate church leaders to take positions on ecclesiastical or social issues and act as spokesmen for the New York church community.

Paul asked him, "If I can come up with a good thirty-minute TV variety program for Christmas, can you get it aired?"

"I'll try," the man replied. "Do you have something you've produced?"

"Not yet," Paul said, smiling, "but we will."

"But Christmas is only four weeks away. Do you have a story, a script? Do you have talent? What about production people?"

"If you will get me a thirty-minute time slot on a New York station, God will help us do the rest!" Paul assured him.

The man shrugged. "I'll try," he said again.

Paul went back to the church's leaders who listened respectfully. They, too, wondered about some of the important elements needed to pull this off.

"That's just it," Paul reminded them. "This whole thing is absolutely impossible without God. Humanly speaking, we have a foot in the door because we might be able to get free air time. And we've got a few things going for us because we have quite a few talented artist-type people in our church. But we have no experienced TV director, no film crew or production people, and—most importantly—no money. The only way this will succeed will be by God's making it happen!"

The church immediately "took" to the idea. Shortly after Paul presented the project to them, he heard back from his media contact. "I've talked to Dick Hughes, vice president and general manager of WPIX-TV. You've got a guarantee of thirty minutes to be broadcast Christmas Eve," he told an elated Paul. "Oh, one other thing," the media man said. "Dick Hughes said you could have two hours of studio time to videotape this show. That's something I never would have counted on. That's gotta be worth a couple thousand dollars. And there's no charge."

"Praise God," answered Paul, who then took the news to the church committee in charge of the project.

"I know we have our backs against the wall. But it's forcing us to trust God to make it happen. Let's give Him whatever help *we* can, but let's allow Him to work in the lives and hearts of others so this idea becomes a reality to them and a testimony to New York of His goodness and greatness," Paul told them. "If you're a writer, give us script ideas. If you're an artist, send us set designs. If you're an actor or actress or musician, tell us what you can do in the program."

The committee began to function. Cheryl Cooper wrote a theatrical sketch for some of the resident acting talent to perform. Effie Jansen composed a theme song for the opening of the show. The Big Apple Corps, a twelve voice choral group, The Manhattan Project vocal group, guitarist Gail Swain, and a small company of acting and musical talent conceived a program format.

"We've got a great program lined up," reported Wayne Rogers. "We've tried to design it to make use of the studio time the station offered us. But—"

Paul looked up from his desk.

". . . we feel that in order to really present this right, we ought to do a filmed opening and drop-in sequence on location. You know, Central Park, Fifth Avenue, places people know and would respond to."

"Sounds good to me," Paul said. "What's the problem."

"Well, there are two problems. To do this right, we'd need a film crew and a director. We'd have to hire them," Wayne said.

"And?" Paul asked.

"Well, a director we could hire for maybe a couple thousand dollars to do both the week of remote filming and the studio production. And I've priced a film crew. Even a small set-up would be somewhere between ten and twenty thousand dollars," Wayne said sadly.

"Why do you want the filmed sequences?" Paul asked.

"Well, when we first discussed it, we felt that it would add much more in production value and 'class.' Instead of the usual 'sermonette' quality, we could honor the Lord with real integrity and professionalism," Wayne explained.

"I believe God is worthy of that extra quality. We will be honoring Him and the birth of His Son with this telecast. We can't afford to treat it in any way but professionally."

"But Paul," Wayne interrupted, "I've just said it will cost probably $25,000 to do it that way. We can't afford it. We simply don't have that kind of money."

"I know," Paul agreed. "But let's pray for another solution. Let's plan to do the filming. I don't know *how,* especially since we have less than three weeks to do it. But let's continue to trust God for a miracle!"

Later that week, at the Bible study meeting, Paul introduced himself to a new convert. "I'm Paul Moore . . . glad you could come."

"Thanks, Reverend. This is kinda new for me. I mean, church and Bible study."

"What's your name, friend?"

"Mike . . . Michael Amber. I'm in film and television."

"Oh?" Paul's eyebrows raised in curiosity. "What do you do?"

"I'm a director," Mike replied.

"Well, you'll be happy to know that you're the first half of an answered prayer." Paul grinned and told him the story of their project. Mike agreed to help as he was able.

The church was encouraged to continue in prayer for the rest of the need—money to film the outdoor sequences. With only two and a half weeks remaining, there was a sense of urgency in their prayers.

In the middle of the week Paul got a long distance telephone call from Mary Latham in Kansas City. She was with the Radio-TV Committee of the Church of the Nazarene.

"Paul, we want to film a report on the urban missions project there in New York for our denominational board meetings and TV spots. I feel terrible about calling you on such short notice. We'd like to film right away, within the next week. Can you help us?"

Paul's mind jumped ahead of her project. "Sure, we can give

you whatever you want. We'd be happy to drop everything. But I have a favor to ask of *you*. Is the film crew busy on the weekend?"

Mary thought for a moment," I don't think so. We planned to finish up there and let them rest in New York for the weekend, then go on to another project. Why?"

Paul explained his need for one or two days use of an experienced, professional film crew. Mary told him she would have to discuss the matter with others at headquarters and call him back.

Mary called back even before Paul could organize a prayer meeting for the consideration. The answer was yes!

In the course of the next week, church members wrote and mimeographed scripts, staged and choreographed sequences, printed huge cue cards, contacted the parks department and police to use locales, set up barricades, and produce the filmed vignettes.

Other church members helped the film crew capture the urban highlights for the mission report and prepare for the weekend production.

Saturday morning dawned sunny (another answer to prayer), and everything was in place. Police barricades kept curious crowds out of camera range while the musicians "lip-synched" prerecorded music and paced out the choreographed routines.

A double-decker English-type bus had been rented for color and atmosphere. The musicians were supposed to get off the bus when it pulled up beside Paul Moore. However, at the last minute John Hillyer made a suggestion: "Paul, would it be okay if we had a celebrity get off the bus and greet you and the TV audience. I think I can get him to do a cameo appearance free."

"Sure, of course, it's a great idea. Who is it?"

But instead of answering, John ran off down the sidewalk, not wanting to keep the film crew standing around. "I saw him at breakfast in the restaurant down the street. Go ahead and shoot that sequence. I'll see if I can get him!" John shouted over his shoulder.

True to his word, John returned within a few minutes and ushered the man aboard the bus.

"Scene five, take one!" called out a young man holding the clap board. Cameras were rolling and the sound man waved that his tape recorder and microphones were ready.

"Action—wave the bus to go!" called Mike Amber.

The double-decker bus, parked a half-block away, drove up and stopped on cue. The doors opened and a tall, broad shouldered man with a tanned and weathered face known to millions stepped off and shook hands with Paul. "Hi, Parson! I'm John Wayne. Happy to see you!"

He then turned to the cameras and introduced Paul and the telecast, saying, "I hope you'll watch this great program of the beautiful Christmas season that has so much meaning to us all."

John Wayne's introducing the "Good News" TV special by the Manhattan Church of the Nazarene was an added touch none of them had even prayed about. Yet, all of the church knew that this project was somehow quite special.

WPIX-TV aired the program on Christmas Eve as promised, and the special was rebroadcast on Christmas Day. Millions of people in New York City and surrounding areas were able to watch it, as were thousands more in New England, upstate New York, Pennsylvania, and New Jersey because of cable TV outlets that carried WPIX-TV signals.

In January, as Paul reviewed the effort with church members, he pointed out that a miracle had taken place.

"I've been told by people who ought to know that we performed something impossible. We were given TV time and use of a studio by the major independent television station in the country. God supplied us with a director, film crew, and even a guest star. They tell me that the kind of production we proposed would cost us maybe $25,000 for broadcast time and studios and another $50,000 for film crew, equipment rental, director, writers, and talent. That doesn't even include John Wayne's fee for a cameo appearance. He donated his time, which was probably worth at least $10,000—*if* you could get him. We're talking about a production that *should* have cost between $75,000 and $100,000! Our only out-of-pocket expense was $200. Now that's what I call a miracle!"

Encouraged by this experience, the people of the Manhattan Church began to stretch their faith in even more areas, trusting God for other "impossible" situations.

By summer, several exciting new ministries were under way. One of them was the "Manhattan Church Movie Reviews." Paul had noticed that, unlike small town or suburban theaters, Manhattan movie houses always played to packed audiences. Even on week nights, long lines of up to two thousand people waited for the next showing.

Paul conceived of a unique witnessing approach to these long lines of people whom church members passed regularly on their way to witness in the singles bars. He suggested that the actors and writers in the church collaborate on a written movie review to hand out to the movie-goers.

The writers went to see the films, then reviewed them thoughtfully. They told of the director's good or bad points, highlighted acting strengths and weaknesses, and commented on the story line or technical aspects of the film. However, each review was written from the philosophical point of view of Christianity. Since most films were not consistent with this viewpoint, the movies generally raised questions that were not answered for the viewer. The movie reviews dealt with those questions and provided Christian answers. The church obtained photos and "mechanicals" so that each review was accompanied by the actual movie logo and artwork.

The flyers contained a brief statement saying that the reviews were produced by a group of young adults on the East Side who were finding answers to life's questions. Included was an invitation to visit the Manhattan Church.

Paul learned that by sending four people with two thousand movie review flyers to the fronts of theaters five minutes before the next showing began, a copy could be given to each person standing in line as well as to all those leaving the theater. In less than fifteen minutes, they could pass along two thousand copies of vital Christian literature that really got read. Almost none were thrown away. Even the managers and ushers of the theaters were impressed with the idea and the quality of the reviews. They even helped pass out the flyers.

Another ministry launched about the same time was similar in that it strategically used contemporary Christian literature. In street corner evangelism, concerts in the parks, and events at the church where young people and children were attracted, the teams distributed "Christian comic books." This series, along with the cartoon versions of famous Christian life stories of such people as Tom Skinner, Corrie Ten Boom, and others, was used most effectively. Through the philanthropy of artist Al Hartley, creator of the "Archie" Christian comic book series, thousands of these illustrated magazines were given away. They were also distributed to kids at the annual Macy's Thanksgiving Day Parade.

The church started a third ministry that likewise grew out of a desire to relate to people on the level of their needs and experiences. Wayne Rogers, one of the charter members of the Manhattan Church, met two beautiful nineteen-year-old models outside the church one day and invited them to church. One of them, a tall, slender fashion model named Jo Ellen, had grown up in Columbus, Ohio, and had come to New York to pursue her career. Jo Ellen did come to church the next Sunday and continued to come. She received Christ and was led with Wayne to start the Inner Light Gospel Cafe. It fast became the most effective outreach to the affluent young adults in the neighborhood. On Saturday nights, well over one hundred people relaxed over dinner and listened to Christian entertainment—usually a rock band, soloist, or another performing group. The Inner Light Gospel Cafe became a place where Christians could invite friends who would otherwise not come to church. In the nonthreatening atmosphere of a supper club, these guests were exposed to Christian fellowship, entertainment, and brief gospel statements meant to attract them to the church on Sunday.

Because God had laid the groundwork and because the fledgling church had waited for Him to act—all the while trusting the ideas and dreams His Spirit had put into their heads—the "impossible" became possible. As the church people trusted Him, miracles began to happen.

Twenty-seven

PAUL WAS WORKING in his office in the Methodist church basement when he was interrupted by a knock on the door. He looked up as he said, "Come in."

The door opened and a tall, heavy man weighing about three hundred pounds filled the door frame. He was about thirty, somewhat unkempt, with long, uncombed hair and a beard.

"Reverend Moore?" he asked hesitantly. At first the man didn't recognize Paul. He had been accustomed to seeing Paul in his traditional garb of denims and clerical collar. However, with changes in the style and approach to the New York ministry, Paul had started wearing a more common suit and tie, and his hair was quite a bit shorter.

"Yes, I'm Paul Moore. How can I help you?"

"Do you remember me? I'm Bob. I stayed with you last year for a couple days."

Paul did remember indeed. He and Sharon had allowed a young couple to stay in their home last year. It was shortly thereafter that their house had been broken into and ransacked. Later, Bob had shown up about the time the Sunday offering was stolen and their house was ransacked again.

At the time, Paul did not associate the two break-ins with the coincidence of Bob's presence. But the second break-in was done by someone who knew (perhaps through the church newsletter) that Paul and Sharon would not be home.

"Yes, Bob . . . I remember you. Where've you been lately?"

"Uh . . . I've been going to church with the Jesus People over in West Patterson."

"Good. How are things with you and the Lord?" Paul asked the big man.

"Okay, I guess. Though my luck seems to be a little lean right now. I need a job and a place to live. I thought you might help me."

"I don't know if we can help or not, Bob. Let me see what I can do, okay? Let me make a few phone calls. You want to wait outside the office? There are some chairs out there."

Bob lumbered out and shut the door. Paul stared at the door for a moment, then picked up the phone and buzzed Michael Christensen (back for another summer intern assignment) on the intercom line. "Mike, keep that big guy out there from leaving while I check him out. I think he might be the one who ripped us off."

Outside, on the extension, Mike looked at the giant sitting in the chair by his desk. He gulped and mumbled, "Okay, Paul."

In his office, Paul immediately thumbed through his personal phone directory and called a friend, the minister of the Jesus People group in West Patterson.

"Do you know a big fella named Bob? He says he's been staying with you guys over there?"

"Yes, Paul. But let me warn you. I don't think Bob is genuine. In fact, when he was here, we had some trouble," the man on the telephone said.

"What kind of trouble?" Paul asked.

"Stealing. We had some things and some money ripped off. No one saw it happen, but we think Bob did it."

"I see," Paul mused. "Anything else?"

"Well, yes," the man hesitated, then spoke, "maybe you ought to know that we checked on Bob. We learned that he's an escaped convict. He's wanted by the authorities for escaping from a Danhurst, Massachusetts, penitentiary."

"Okay, thanks very much," Paul said as he hung up.

Outside Paul's office, Bob began to shift his bulk nervously on the metal folding chair. Mike looked over at him, not as concerned about whether the chair could hold the fat man as much as whether *he* could if Bob got suspicious and ran.

Only a few minutes had elapsed since Paul buzzed him, but it seemed much longer to Mike. Finally Paul's door opened, and he strode out with anger in his eyes.

The staff had never seen Paul angry before.

"You dirty, no-good bum!" Paul shouted.

Bob looked up with a confused, pained look.

"You were the guy who broke in and ripped us off! Weren't you?" Paul continued.

The three-hundred pound hulk lowered his head, feeling a mixture of shame and relief for having been found out. He nodded slowly.

"Why? How could you do such a miserable rotten thing?"

Mike and a secretary were watching Paul's verbal assault on the fugitive. They were a bit fearful of what might happen, and the secretary picked up the phone to dial for help if it were needed.

Paul's anger was rising. "You stole the coin collection I had since I was a *kid!* My dad and I worked on that collection for fifteen *years,* man. And you probably gave those coins away for a bag of dope!"

Bob's sullen expression changed to one of contrition. His big shoulders drooped and began to shake as he began to cry. But Paul did not let up. He paced around the chair, shaking his finger at the thief. "You couldn't even pick the lock—you had to break down the whole blasted door! I had to pay for a new door besides losing my stuff!"

The man was sobbing loudly now.

"And you wrecked my wife's clothes," Paul continued. "You ripped up her clothes looking for stuff. That's really crummy!" Paul lashed out angrily at the big man as if Bob represented all the cosmic powers of evil, all the stress and tensions, all the forces fighting against them since they had come to New York.

Mike was beginning to feel sorry for the crook now. "Paul, maybe he's had enough."

Paul, suddenly alert to his anger, stopped in midsentence. Then he said, his voice more controlled, "Okay. Bob, you wait in that Sunday school room while we decide what to do."

Like a whipped child, Bob did as he was told.

"What are you going to do with him?" Mike asked.

"I dunno. He's an escaped convict. He escaped from the

penitentiary in Massachusetts. We can't keep him here. We'd be harboring a fugitive."

"And we can't very well give him some money and send him on his way," Mike added.

"Maybe he's under conviction. He seemed genuinely sorry," Paul mused. "I guess we'll have to pray about it. We can try to get him to give himself up, but I don't know if he will."

"Well, for sure we should pray about this," Mike agreed.

"Yeah . . . do you think we *should* forgive him and send him on his way?" Paul asked. "Do you think my whole attitude was un-Christian?"

"Uh . . . well, not really. It's just . . . uh . . . well, he came here looking for help and . . . uh . . . you came down on him pretty hard," Mike said awkwardly.

"I guess I was mad 'cause he stole from us. Well, let's pray about it, okay?" Paul smiled.

Before they could do so, however, the basement was suddenly and noisily invaded by several uniformed policemen with guns drawn and nightsticks ready.

"Somebody call about a fugitive?" one of them bellowed.

Mike and Paul looked at each other questioningly. They then noticed the frightened secretary, half-cowering behind her desk, pointing to the Sunday school room where Bob was waiting.

The cops barged into the room and surprised the big man. His eyes widened in fear as they rushed him and wrestled him to the floor. Quickly one of the officers clamped Bob's hands behind him and snapped on handcuffs. He jammed the night stick under his hands and the two of them yanked Bob clumsily to his feet.

As they spun him around to take him away, Paul saw the hurt and feelings of betrayal in Bob's eyes.

Before the policemen escorted Bob outside to the waiting squad car, Paul quickly stepped over to Bob. "I'm sorry. This isn't what we wanted. We planned to pray first about what to do."

Bob said nothing, but gazed down, beaten.

For several minutes after they left, the staff sat there quietly. Then they prayed, asking especially for guidance.

Paul came up with an idea. "Let's go down and sign a complaint. If we press charges here in New York, they probably won't extradite him to Massachusetts to serve his sentence. If we sign complaints, that way they'll keep him here to start trial. At least we can minister to him then."

It happened just that way. Bob pleaded guilty to the burglary charge and was sentenced to six months in jail. Meanwhile, Paul and members of the church went to visit Bob regularly. The big man seemed to genuinely repent of his crimes and prayed that God would change his life.

III. The Lamb's Club

Twenty-eight

ABOUT A YEAR after the Manhattan Church was chartered, Paul Moore and the congregation learned about the new leader in the district.

Reverend M. V. Scutt was appointed to replace Reverend Jack White. He immediately sought to build a bridge of communication between Paul and himself and spent many of his first days as New York district superintendent in Manhattan, walking the streets with Paul, witnessing, and seeing firsthand what was happening.

Reverend Scutt was an athletic man about forty—a tall ex-marine with short hair. He was well dressed, exceptionally neat, and carried himself with a confident military bearing. He was a church leader who was going to play by the rules, Paul learned. Reverend Scutt listened, but weighed his words very carefully before saying anything. Paul began the process of getting to know him. Because of the enormous shadow cast by Jack White who preceded him, it would be some time before Reverend Scutt won Paul's full respect and confidence.

About the same time, the Manhattan Church of the Nazarene was becoming more visible in the community. The summer park concerts, comic book and movie review literature evangelism, "Inner Light Gospel Cafe," and regular worship services were known to many on the Upper East Side.

Probably the one event that gave them greatest visibility was the "campaign" Paul launched in September, 1974, in opposition to the South Korean cult leader, the Reverend Sun Myung Moon. *Time, Newsweek, The New York Times, Christianity Today,* and all the New York TV and newspaper media covered the confrontation.

Reverend Moon, a self-proclaimed "prophet" came to the United States to recruit followers, many of whom would come to regard Moon as a messiah, a successor to Jesus Christ.

Moon and his followers spent an estimated $350,000 on local radio, TV, billboard, and newspaper advertising to promote a giant rally in Madison Square Garden.

"We've go to do something," Paul told his staff after reading about the planned rally. "This Moon guy is a liar and deceiver! He has denied many of the basic Christian doctrines. He denies the need of salvation and its reality through Christ's death on the cross. He doesn't believe in the Trinity or the inspiration of Scriptures. And he even encourages his followers to believe in him, rather than Jesus, as the Lord of the Second Coming. He's a fraud, yet he still calls himself a Christian!"

The small group discussed ideas on how to effectively oppose the Moon rally. Several daring but creative ideas emerged, and before long they had an agenda.

"This project is too big for our church. We've got to mobilize some help," Paul observed. Within a few days he had called fifty other New York churches, many of which joined him to organize a coalition of "Christians United for Jesus as Lord." This group, led by Paul, began to train nearly 350 Christian demonstrators. Their goal was to "take on" Reverend Moon and his followers and disrupt or discredit the planned rally.

Paul knew the press would be watching the Moon-sponsored event. Paul's strategy was to counter that media coverage with the truth about Moon's deceptions regarding Christianity. The demonstrations and disruptions would cause the media to ask about the opposition, and Paul could explain the purpose of the church coalition.

Paul organized the protest almost as a guerrilla campaign. The 350 Christian volunteers were assigned to various "squads," "platoons," and "companies." The leaders of the units were "lieutenants," "captains," "majors," "colonels," and "generals."

Some of the "squads" had individuals assigned to distribute anti-Moon literature, disguised as Moon's own materials and using his logo and slogan, "September 18 could be your rebirthday." "We'll have seven vans loaded with literature constantly circling the block to replenish supplies if squads run out or if one or two have a small supply confiscated," Paul explained.

Joel Tucciarone visited a small Chinese bakery in one of New York's oriental neighborhoods. "Can you make me some fortune cookies with my own message printed inside?" he asked.

"Yes," the Chinese baker answered. "How many do you want?"

"I want two thousand by September 17," Joel said.

The baker shrugged. "They will be ready."

Later Paul met with his "generals" to go over details. "The American Bible Society is going to give us twenty thousand copies of the Gospel of Luke to hand out. This along with the fifty thousand tracts we've had printed should be given to everyone who comes," he told them.

"We'll have two forces," Paul continued. "A major confrontation force and guerrilla infiltrators. The confrontation people will use battery-operated bullhorns at each entrance to the Garden, declaring "Jesus is Lord—Not Mr. Moon." Pickets with signs will march up and down.

"We also have several 'squads' of Korean Christians, dressed in native costumes," Paul added. "The women in their oriental gowns will be mistaken for Moon's Korean Folk Ballet troupe. They will work their way to the front of the Garden and, when everyone is seated, pull out hidden packets of literature. They'll look like Moon's people passing out literature; before our people are discovered and tossed out, we should be able to get a copy to every person inside."

Paul pointed to a chart that revealed in elaborate detail the Madison Square Garden floor plan. "We have a wealthy Christian friend who has rented a private VIP box up here. We can squeeze one hundred people into that box, along with the cartons of literature. They'll disperse from the box seats at just the right moment."

"Ingenious," someone commented.

"Maybe," Paul cautioned, "but none of it will succeed without careful planning, absolute timing, and much prayer."

On the day of the rally, Paul learned that Moon's supporters were taking no chances about having a crowd show up. "They've handed out 380,000 free tickets for only twenty thousand seats in the Garden. They're bound to have a turn-away crowd," he said. "How fast can we print up ten thousand handbills?"

"I know a place where we could get them in time—but that's with typesetting all done," Mike replied.

"Well, find a typesetter who'll do it while you wait." Paul grabbed a sheet of paper and sketched a quick layout announcing the "Sun Myung Moon Overflow Concert."

"Mark, call the Glad Tidings Tabernacle. They're just a block away. See if they'll let us put on a concert there tonight. Then, work with Mike to put it together. Bob DiQuattro and Sharon will set up the music end of it. We'll feature the Manhattan Project and our band. We don't have much time, so get right on it!" Paul ordered.

That night, in addition to the Christians United group, several hundred political demonstrators were also on hand to picket Moon, charging that he was a "fascist" who supported a South Korean "dictatorship." Many of Moon's "security" people were busy trying to deal with the disruptions caused by the political demonstrators. Paul's "troops," drilled and committed, executed their orders with precision.

Outside Madison Square Garden, the attention of Moon's people was divided between the hundreds of political protestors and the picketing, placard-waving Christians United supporters. As planned, hundreds of "infiltrators" carried out their sabotage and disruption. The corps had now grown to four hundred Christians countering the Moon rally.

Joel Tucciarone had typed the lines "Jesus is Lord—not Mr. Moon" on a sheet of paper several hundred times and ran off copies. These were cut into strips and put into the fortune cookies. Laboriously, he and volunteers created an "assembly line" of placing one cookie in a small plastic bag and stapling it closed. These were all handed out in several minutes time by Korean Christians in oriental costumes.

The literature was distributed quickly and efficiently, also. Thousands of people read a pamphlet with Moon's slogan on the outside; but inside, the pages told readers to "accept Jesus Christ as your Savior—don't settle for Moonshine!" Only a few of those distributing tracts or Gospel portions were "captured" and hustled out of the Garden. But even those who were caught would simply flag down one of the seven secretly marked vans circling the block and replenish his supply, often going back into the Garden through a different entrance.

Paul stationed a group of highly visible pickets across the street from the Garden. Not lost in the milling crowds, they were easily seen by the New York TV and newspaper people. As spokesman, Paul was able to articulate his objections to Reverend Moon and his spurious teachings. By keeping his replies brief, dramatic, and to the point, Paul knew he was assured of his statement's being used on the seven o'clock news and in *Time* magazine.

As expected, a capacity crowd forced police to close the Garden's doors early. Thousands of angry people were left milling outside. Using handbills printed only two hours before and the bullhorn systems, the Christians United people directed the crowd to the nearby Glad Tidings Tabernacle.

The crowd, sensing that many would be turned away from this event also, turned and literally *ran* to the church a block away. Paul closed the doors after a thousand people pressed tightly into the church. People began to pound on the door angrily with their fists. Paul went outside and grabbed a bullhorn.

"Please be patient! We'll have another concert for you in an hour. The building is packed! We can't let you inside—there's no room. But we'll have another concert inside soon."

The entire operation went smoothly. After the first concert, scores came forward to receive Christ. There were another thouand people waiting to get into the second concert, with similar results after the music and gospel message.

Inside the Garden, only half of Moon's audience stayed to hear him preach for two and one-half hours. All in all, the campaign was a victory for a dedicated group of Christian soldiers.

 Twenty-nine

THERE WAS HARDLY time for inventory following the Christians United campaign before Paul was planning the church's next project.

Born-again artists, actors, actresses, writers, and musicians had found a church home in the Manhattan Church of the Nazarene. After coming to Christ, they wanted to express themselves and use their artistic gifts in some Christ-centered form of communication. Some of them found fulfillment in singing and playing or giving dramatic readings or theatrical monologues in church or at the Inner Light Gospel Cafe.

However, Paul had challenged them to "resurrect the arts—through the power of Christ's resurrection." It began as a seed-thought planted within the artistic imagination of the congregation and took shape several months later as "A New Way of Living," a two and one-half hour multi-media spectacular.

The New York Christian Theater grew from that same first seed-thought. This drama company wrote, produced, and performed contemporary "parables" as part of the presentation. The Manhattan Project, along with Effie Jansen, provided music.

However, the central focus of "A New Way of Living" was a giant three-screen, multi-media visual display programmed by a computer. It began with composer Ferde Grofe's "Sunrise," a musical masterpiece from his famous *Grand Canyon Suite*. On screen, a panorama of New York City at dawn was shown, depicting the Manhattan skyline as the sun rose over the city.

The pictures dissolved and changed with the music. As the tempo increased, so did the activity of the streets of New York—with commuters, shoppers, panhandlers, and taxi cabs rushing to meet the new day. Other scenes showed the poor and lonely wanderers in the city, the lost and forgotten. As the New York "day" progressed on screen, neon corridors led to Manhattan by night, with its brilliant and enticing night spots and sinful attractions. Then as a transition, the visuals showed a woman, leaving behind the scenes of New York night life and sitting down to play at a huge piano. Suddenly, the three screens went dark, the stage lights blazed on, and the audience saw Effie Jansen, the woman on screen seconds before, now "live" and seated at the piano to perform in person.

Paul preached in parable as part of the presentation. The entire work was overwhelming, and after its presentation at Manhattan Church, Paul suggested they plan a nationwide tour and take "A New Way of Living" to other churches, and especially to Christian colleges, "as evidence that God has not abandoned the arts."

He told students and ministers, "For too long the evangelical church has turned its back on the arts. We have said that drama and some of the other expressions of the arts are out of place in the church and that Christians have no place in these fields. "Rather," he said, "I challenge you to redeem the arts as a means of bringing glory to God. Express your gifts of music, painting, sculpture, drama, writing—whatever your talent—in tribute to Him, and do it in the church."

Paul and more than thirty people from the Manhattan Church took that message and the "A New Way of Living" production—with screens, projectors, sound equipment, klieg lights, sets, and costumes—on tour from New York to Columbus, Nashville, Denver, Portland, San Diego, St. Louis, and Chicago.

Audiences in churches and colleges were delighted. The group's vigorous schedule called for them to drive from city to city, unload the heavy cases, set up the equipment, put up sets, rehearse and put on costumes then perform. When the performance was over they had to take down the equipment, load the bus, and drive six hundred miles to the next stop. The back-breaking schedule was outdone only by the "impossible" itinerary. Even for the young performers, the tour was taxing. They covered eight thousand miles coast to coast in nineteen days, with performances in nineteen major cities.

Through it all, their dream of seeing the arts elevated in the eyes of ministers and students was realized. As they performed on Christian campuses, young artists were challenged to "resurrect the arts through the power of the Resurrection" and encouraged to pursue a career in the arts and bring glory to God.

Several churches responded by organizing theater groups of their own. Student leaders told of their appreciation! "Thanks for letting me see that I don't have to leave the church to be creative or go into the world to share in the arts."

While churches around the country demonstrated their gratefulness to Paul for the national tour of the "A New Way of Living" spectacular, there were other churches that expressed, indirectly, their irritation over what they felt were "problem" aspects of Paul's style and ministry.

Paul learned of the criticisms from Reverend Scutt.

There were critics who questioned the contemporary aspects of the music and the visuals of the multi-media presentation. Designed for a collegiate audience, it wasn't as well accepted when it was presented as a program at the district assembly.

There were others in the district who questioned the value of Paul's skirmish with Reverend Moon and the subsequent press coverage. They especially criticized his methods. Still other criticisms concerned the "casual" approach to worship services.

Reverend Scutt knew most of the complaints were made because of general misunderstandings, but he was caught in the middle. He understood why some would complain about the Manhattan Church and its young, aggressive pastor.

He had tried to send Paul signals that such criticisms were likely. Paul, zealous for his own work, paid little attention to denominational events other than those in which he or his church were involved. As a result, to some of his fellow pastors in the district, Paul came off as brash and arrogant. His church, because of the TV coverage and publicity, seemed immature and self-centered to others.

Reverend Scutt could see there were still bridges to build.

Thirty

PETER PASQUALINO WAS waiting for Paul when he got to his office.

"Pastor, I need to talk to you," he said.

"Sure, Pete . . . come on in."

Peter was nervous. His eyes were bloodshot and his clothes disheveled, indicating that he had probably been up all night.

"Is there something wrong, Pete?"

"Yeah, there is, Pastor. Jude and I have split; we're getting a divorce."

Paul was not ready for the shocking news. Peter was one of the twelve daresaints who had reoriented his career in order to help start the Manhattan Church. He and his wife, Jude, had been won to Christ in New Milford, but Jude hadn't been willing to make the move to New York. She felt she had to stay with her father in New Jersey who was dying of cancer. Peter had tried commuting, but Jude became more and more disillusioned with the church and its demands on Peter.

She had stopped coming to church, and soon after that they separated. Now, after futile counselling, she had filed for divorce.

After Peter left, Paul felt his eyes filling with tears. He sat at his desk not knowing what to do. It was as if he'd been slapped. The sting of Peter's words had wounded Paul deeply. He took the news personally and somehow felt responsible.

Why haven't I noticed? I should have ministered to them more directly, he thought.

He went home and told Sharon the news about their friends. She became upset too because of the closeness they had with Pete and Jude.

"They're both hurting very deeply right now," Sharon said.

"I know . . . I can't believe how easily 'divorce' has gotten into our vocabulary. I remember when the church never used the word 'divorce,' " Paul observed.

"There seems to be a lot of other trouble over this same type of casual attitude," Sharon observed. "I just heard today that Peggy is pregnant."

She was referring to an unmarried girl in their congregation. Peggy had witnessed to an unbeliever in a singles bar and had led him to Christ; but over a period of time she had gotten personally involved. Instead of asking one of the men in the church to work with him, Peggy had tried to counsel and lead him into a Christian lifestyle. Unfortunately, his still-permissive lifestyle had influenced her. Paul had suspected that they might be sleeping together, but he had never questioned Peggy about it.

"What's she going to do about it?" Paul asked Sharon.

"I talked to her this afternoon. She confirmed it, and the man she's been counselling is the father. She asked about a place to go to have the baby. She doesn't want an abortion."

"Well, thank God for *that* anyway," Paul remarked. "Remember when Rachel got pregnant this summer and had an abortion against our advice?" Paul recalled a previous incident of sexual promiscuity.

"If Satan can't divide us or defeat us because of our lack of love for one another, he'll do it through the wrong kind of love—you know, promiscuity. There's an awful lot of that in our church, Paul," Sharon remarked.

"Oh, not a *lot*," Paul argued. "I don't think it's all that widespread. But I'll admit, even a little is bad."

Sharon did not dismiss her intuitive fears as easily, though.

The Maranatha Church of the Nazarene in New Milford, New Jersey, consisted mainly of young people, genuine before God, but exuberant in their praise.

One of the creative ways used to attract children to backyard Sunday school classes was the use of Bert, Ernie, and other *Sesame Street* characters.

Charlie Rizzo, a former speed freak and one of the first converts in New Milford, played at the Columbia University meeting when Paul met Bob DiQuattro again.

During the warm summer months, Sunday afternoon services were held in the garden behind the house on East Seventy-second Street.

The Manhattan Project—Sharon Moore, Bob DiQuattro, and Judi Cochran (l to r) sang on the "I Care TV Special."

In the summer of 1973, Rev. Jack White (l) dedicated Paul Moore II while Sheri, Sharon, Paul, and Paul's mother looked on.

A unique ministry is the "Manhattan Church Movie Reviews," which are given out in front of movie theaters.

When the self-proclaimed "prophet" Sun Myung Moon held a rally in Madison Square Garden, Judi Cochran and others were there to say that Jesus is Lord.

The Lamb's Club, the six-story historical landmark in the heart of Times Square that now houses the Manhattan Church of the Nazarene.

The New York Christian Theater Company has performed many plays at the Lamb's Club including *You're a Good Man, Charlie Brown*.

The Sanctuary Restaurant in
The Lamb's is open every day
for lunch and dinner.

In November, 1978, the Crisis Care Center
had a Thanksgiving banquet for street
people—New York's outcasts.

Thousands of young teen prostitutes roam
New York City streets. Lamb's Center for
Girls offers freedom to many.

Pappa John O'Shaughnessey

Joe Colaizzi

Effie Jansen Canapa

Jim Hullinger, Mark Weimer, Joel Tucciarone,
Wayne Rogers (l to r).

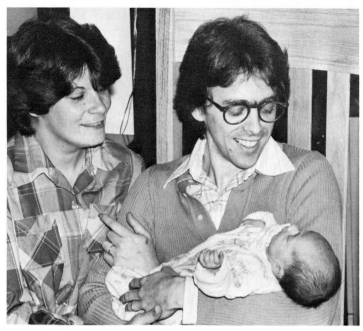

Joyce, Steven, and Molly Mane Suggs

In October, 1975, Treena and Graham Kerr (The Galloping Gourmet) joined Paul for the five-hour prime time "I Care TV Special."

At the center of all the activities of the Lamb's is the preaching of the Word of God every Sunday.

Sheri, Cathi, Paul, Paul II, and Sharon Moore (l to r).

SHEPHERD OF TIMES SQUARE

A week later Paul was awakened in the middle of the night with a phone call. The woman on the other end was angry.

"Pastor, this is Carol Gates. I just want to tell you that you've got *some* kind of church."

Sleepily Paul mumbled, "What's that? Carol, what's the matter?"

"George was out 'witnessing,' " she said with sarcasm, "and he came home drunk again! And when I spoke to him, he started to hit me. I can't *take* this abuse, Mister! How can you justify this and call yourself a minister?"

She slammed the phone down, and Paul, now wide awake, lay listening to the dial tone and staring at the receiver.

Slowly he replaced the phone on the night table and switched off the lamp. In the darkness he thought about the accusation that had just come.

George was a new Christian and a musician for one of the church's music groups. The group had been asked to perform in a night club where it could sing and play a mix of fifty percent pop songs and fifty per cent gospel music.

"It's a one-month contract," the music group's leader had told Paul. "We'll use that time for witnessing to the people in the night club."

But the plan, however fine the motives, did not work. Gospel music, played in such a setting, lost its convicting power. Drunks mocked its message, often singing along or heckling the performers.

The night club owner, knowing about the group's Christian stand, for unknown reasons tried various ways of undermining their witness. He regularly offered drinks to the performers during the breaks. While the rest of the group politely refused, George didn't. One drink led to another . . . and another . . . and soon George was going home drunk.

His wife was right. There was no way to justify this behavior. Paul knew he would not sleep any more this night and began to use the remaining hours for prayer.

He thought about the many "failures" of the past few months:

divorce, illegitimate pregnancies, and now this irresponsible situation with George.

"Lord," he prayed, "I can see I've made some mistakes in judgment. In my desire to see people come to Christ, I've been winking at some of the things that go on as part of their old lifestyles. God, I know that you've called your children to 'come apart and be separate' from the world—to live holy lives. Forgive me for not being a stronger leader and pastor with regard to these matters. Lord, you know our motives were good. But our methods and attitudes need work. I pray you'll reveal to me what we as a church should do."

Paul got up, dressed, and took a stroll along the East River. He often took long walks at night for prayer and meditation. While watching the tugboats and listening to the foghorns, his mind was released from the usual distractions and was free to focus on God's thoughts with greater clarity.

As he continued to pray about disintegration in the lives of some of his flock, Paul began to understand two basic principles.

First, he was reminded that "we wrestle not against powers on earth, but cosmic evil powers." Paul thought again of the oppressive, heavy concentration of evil powers in New York— powers of incredible strength that never go away. The only way to "bind" these powers would be through prayer, fasting, and intercession with God—the greatest Power in the universe.

Secondly, Paul realized that in beginning a church that would not offend New Yorkers, he had winked at their laxity in moral matters.

You are a Wesleyan pastor, Paul reminded himself. *You believe in the sanctity of the life of holiness—the heart made perfect in love; the mind purified by faith that gives us power and victory over sin.*

As Paul strode along the river in the darkness, his mind began to come alive. Thoughts raced and conclusions formed. It was as if the answers had been there all along, just waiting for this moment. Paul hurried home and went inside, trying not to awaken Sharon. He slipped into his den and turned on the light.

Reaching for his Bible and notebook, Paul sat down and began to organize his thoughts into a sermon.

Paul's preaching on Sunday was dynamic—some thought fiery. Many said it was inspired, and more than a few felt its sting and rebuke.

"Please turn to Revelation, chapter two," Paul began. There was a rustle of pages being turned as he continued. "Jesus Christ, through the writer of the Book of Revelation, addressed seven churches in chapters two and three. He thoroughly examined the church to see how it measured up. The risen Lord is always in the best possible position to evaluate the condition of the church . . . to *commend* it, to *criticise* it, and to *command* it to change.

" 'I know all your ways,' says Christ. We try to pull down the shades on our evil, we take such precautions to cover up our sin, and all the time He's right there watching it all—listening to every conversation, weighing every intent of the heart, knowing every secret thought.

"Jesus begins His Word to the churches by *commending* their virtues. He says, 'I know . . . your toil.' The early church was active. It had a 'crisis care center' that ministered to the needy. It possibly had a center for runaway teenage girls. You can be certain the members visited the sick, the lonely, the aged.

"He also commends them for their endurance. 'I know . . . your . . . faithfulness.' The Christians were exposed to fierce opposition because they challenged false religions, and spoke out against idolatry. They learned the cost of starting a church in a hedonistic urban center. Anyone who disapproved of the Emperor was ostracized from his community or, worse yet, killed. Nevertheless, they were faithful in their allegiance to Christ.

"A third virtue for which Christ commends the church is orthodoxy. When others taught serious error, it pursued sound doctrine. 'You did not deny your faith in me,' He says.

"However, the early church had fallen from the heights of devotion to Christ and descended to mediocrity and so He *criticises* it.

You have lost your early love (Rev. 2:5).
You commit fornication (Rev. 2:14).
You are lukewarm (Rev. 3:16).

"Jesus pleads for our love again. He wants to restore to us the 'joy of our salvation.' The church had works—but not love. It had orthodoxy—but not love. Loss of love can be restored by a deeper worship—not hollow songs and phony acts, but by a worshipful lifestyle.

"Jesus pleads for holiness. The church experienced gross sexual immorality under the cloak of piety. The wicked—in as well as out of the church—persuade themselves that their wickedness is not known. But nothing is hidden from God. We cannot escape His gaze, nor should we want to.

"Therefore Christ *commands* the church to repent. He is not going to force us to surrender, but He says, 'I have given her time to repent.' Judgment is only for those who do not repent. But the faithful saint who has repudiated the standards of the world and who by the Spirit controls the desires of the flesh and surrenders himself to the cleansing flame of Pentecost will share both Christ's authority and Christ's glory. The faithful saint must 'throw off . . . every sin to which we cling.'

"No matter what the sin to which you cling is, you may be sure that true deliverance will not come unless you *hate* it.

"The gay controlled by lust will never be free until he hates his sin enough to break up housekeeping with his male lover, until he hates his sin enough to stop going to gay bars, until he hates his sin enough to change his wardrobe to avoid identification with the gay world. He must hate his sin enough to submit himself to discipleship from a heterosexually oriented, spirit-filled man.

"The immoral, unmarried couple, trapped in this permissive society that sanctions premarital and extramarital sex, must hate their sin enough to stop taking the pill ('just in case'), must hate their sin enough to stop buying filthy pornographic literature, must hate their sin enough to stop spending time together alone in each other's apartment.

"Until the gossiper, who sits in his vacuum of idleness, waiting to suck up the first rumor of carnal criticism that comes along, hates his sin, he will never be free. Nor will the liar or the idolator. Those who claim to have received the heavenly gift, yet go on sinning, '. . . with their own hands they are crucifying the Son of God and making mock of His death' (Heb. 6:6).

"Hate sin! Despise lust, immorality, gossip, false doctrine, lying, idolatry, pride. And beloved, it is only as you turn your back on the darkness of sin that you will see the light of the glory of God in the matchless face of Jesus Christ.

"Remember that *holiness* was the missing quality in the church. The church may have had activities, endurance, and great faith, but they condoned immoral conduct. 'This is the will of God, that you should be holy . . .' (1 Thess. 4:3). God is calling you to holiness right now."

The sermon brought immediate reactions as well as long-term results. Genuine, tearful repentance and revival began with the prayer following Paul's sermon, and many people went to the front of the church to indicate their conviction and decision to change.

The service marked the turning point in the congregation's maturity and discipline. Paul's emphasis in this sermon and the one's that followed was not so much to preach *against* sin as to preach *for* holiness.

Many of the issues Paul had referred to in his sermons were corrected at once as people went forward in church, or later repented alone on their knees before God.

A few, however, did not see things as being so black and white. One man had been dating a married woman. "But she is waiting for her divorce so we can be married. Her husband is an unbeliever and ran out on her. We're both Christians and love the Lord. Accept us as we are," he announced, "or we'll leave the church."

"If you love the Lord," Paul counselled gently, "you wouldn't do something that offends and hurts Him deeply. Please pray about it, Jerry."

The couple left the church but called several months later to apologize. "I'm sorry, Pastor. You were right. God has convicted us for not holding to His values. We've decided not to see each other until after her divorce is final, and then only if He leads us back together."

Another man, a homosexual who had lapsed into his past lifestyle, later came to Paul for counselling.

"God only asks you to repent. All you have to do is forsake immorality and He's pomised to restore you," Paul told him.

In addition to a call to holiness standards among the people, the church elders also began to deal with matters of church discipline that had been ignored before. Bob DiQuattro, one of their most gifted leaders, resigned from his position on the church board because he wanted to get his personal life "squared away." The elders agreed on account of his back and forth attitude regarding his divorce. On one occasion Bob would ask his friends to pray for Esther to come back to him. The next time, he would seem to have accepted the divorce as final and was dating other women.

"The Scriptures are clear, Bob," the elders told him. You have to stop seeing other women if you really want a reconciliation. Or, you need to know that you have been released by Esther, that there's no hope for a reconciliation. If you think it's possible for God to intervene and get you and Esther back together, you've got to show good faith and stop seeing other women."

When Bob decided to seriously seek reconciliation with Esther, Paul and the board of elders affirmed Bob in his decision and supported him with prayer and encouragement. They all knew it would take a miracle after two years of separation. But after all, doesn't God delight in "impossibilities"?

Thirty-one

WINTER WAS APPROACHING in New York, but in an apartment in Cali, Colombia, where Esther DiQuattro had taken a job as a secretary, temperatures were sweltering.

Esther sat beside a small table and reread the two letters from the United States. One was from the attorney she and her mother had hired to handle the divorce proceedings against Bob. The letter advised Esther that the decree was final. She was now divorced from Bob DiQuattro.

Divorced. The word had unusual finality. Was this really what she wanted? Esther wasn't sure. *Perhaps if Bob had made more of an effort to understand. . .*

And why hadn't he written? Esther's eyes clouded over as she thought of Bob. *Why can't I get him out of my mind?*

Esther wondered if Bob's letters had been lost or intercepted before reaching her. There was, in fact, one letter from Bob. It was the second one lying on the table. It had arrived suddenly and mysteriously almost a year ago. A member of the Fellowship had gone back to New York City for a brief visit. Unknown to Esther, this man had talked to Bob. The man had returned to South America and delivered the letter to her. It was brief and to the point. Bob told of his emptiness the past several years and of his hope that somehow God would reunite them. He concluded the note with a simple plea: *"I still love you! Please write."*

Esther had never told anyone about that mysterious letter. But now, as she held Bob's note in one hand and the divorce decree in the other, she began to consider his words deeply.

SHEPHERD OF TIMES SQUARE

Icy winter slush splashed over the curb as a Manhattan taxi sped around the corner. Wayne Rogers, Mark Weimer, and Paul jumped back to avoid the spray. The three were walking down Forty-second Street, nearing Times Square.

Mark was from San Jose, California, and never really felt warm enough in New York during the winter months. Paul had recruited Mark when the "A New Way of Living" group went to the West Coast. Paul had been made aware of Mark's exceptional leadership qualities and managerial skills earlier and asked him to come to New York and help him in key areas. Since Mark had started and run a television ministry over cable TV in northern California, Paul was interested in using these skills in his own CATV ministry on Manhattan Cable TV.

As the three walked along, they discussed the previous night's New Years's Eve supper party in the Inner Light Cafe at the Methodist church. In the middle of the celebration, the Christians were interrupted by loud cursing and drunken screaming. At first, Paul thought it was a drunk from the street, coming in for warmth and losing control. However, it was a woman socialite, a neighbor from the prestigious town house next door. "I've had it with you people!" she screamed. Her words were followed by a stream of the most vulgar cursing imaginable. Immediately, heads bowed all over the room, and subdued but audible prayers were offered.

"We don't want you here, you bunch of ---!"

Paul winced as the woman continued her tirade; then, shaking her fist threateningly, she turned and left.

Walking along the street now, Paul could still feel the sting of her obscenities and screams. "Men," he said to Wayne and Mark, "it's plain to me that we'll have a continuing run-in with this woman and the other tenants in the building next door. Then, too, some of the older people in the Methodist church are complaining to their pastor about us. We're too noisy, too different. I'll bet it won't be long before *they'll* want us out. We should start looking for a new building. I think we ought to have a place of our own. We can't work out something on a shared basis if half the people are afraid you're going to wear out their building because you use amplifiers and loud music."

"Well," Wayne observed, "why don't we look for our own place, something we wouldn't have to share with someone else?"

"Good idea," Mark offered.

Paul nodded. "Being in someone else's church is like wearing someone else's clothes; you're glad you're covered, but you never really feel comfortable."

It had already become uncomfortable. As the services attracted more people on Sunday, the crowds grew too large for the basement facilities but were still much too small for the sanctuary upstairs. Nor could they hold regular Sunday morning worship services because the original congregation used it then.

The cable television productions were curtailed because of constant scheduling hassles. The actors and actresses of the newly formed New York Christian Theater were restricted by the facilities as to what they could produce or perform.

"We're to the place where we'll *have* to move in order to keep growing," Paul told them.

It all seemed so hopeless. As Bob DiQuattro returned to his apartment one night he felt the wave of grief, the knot in his chest that returned whenever he thought of his ex-wife. If she had died, he could have dealt with the grief. The hurt would have healed in time. But her loss through divorce remained an unhealed wound. He did not know quite how to cope with these feelings.

He'd tried to share them with his Christian friends in the Manhattan Church. With the revival and spiritual maturity resulting from Paul's sermons and emphasis on holiness the previous fall, there had come a new spirit of prayer and caring. In place of attitudes of condemnation, the people were showing genuine prayerful concern. Friends in church were praying for Bob and Esther, though many of them—even the charter members of the Manhattan Church—had never met her.

Bob was grateful for their love and prayers. It reinforced his own wobbly faith many times to hear them ask God for what would sound silly and unrealistic to those less spiritually mature.

Bob emptied his mail box and started toward his apartment door. Suddenly, he caught his breath and felt dizzy. He looked at a small envelope in his hand. It was postmarked from South America. The address was written in a familiar handwriting.

"Esther!" he shouted. Tearing open the letter, he quickly read its contents. Then he read them again. For several moments he stood outside in the hall studying the letter.

She said simply, "Yes, we need to get together and make peace with each other. I think I still love you too."

It didn't take long at all for the news to circulate through the church. People who had been praying saw Esther's letter as evidence that their prayers were being answered.

"But I don't know if she wants to get back together," Bob said. "The divorce is final; I've been praying we'd get back together, but all I know at this point is that she still thinks of me. That's a place to start!"

"Call her, Bob," someone suggested. "Don't trust the mail. See if she'll meet you some place halfway to talk things over."

It was done so quickly that none of them quite believed it was happening. Bob reached Esther and both could sense that, in spite of the miles between them, there was still a love and closeness. They agreed to fly to Orlando to meet and discuss a reconciliation, their tickets paid for through a "love offering" provided by the Manhattan Church.

Paul watched as an anxious Bob DiQuattro left for the airport. "God still has plenty of miracles left, doesn't He?" Paul said with a smile, extending his hand.

 # Thirty-two

WAYNE ROGERS AND Paul were having one of their early morning staff meetings to discuss progress about a new church building.

"We need a place to worship where we won't have to schedule around another congregation," Paul commented. "We need a place that's sort of 'neutral' so we can offer dramatic programs and concerts and start the Inner Light Gospel Cafe again. If we have a neutral place, not necessarily a church, we might attract more non-Christians. The ferry boat might have worked, but God closed that door."

"Well," Wayne replied, "what about a place with all that, plus plenty of rooms for residences and offices?"

"You've found a place?" Paul asked.

Wayne's eyes sparkled. "You know how we've been praying and trusting God for just the right place? We've said, 'God, You know our needs better than we do.' Well, I believe He's led us to that place!"

"Really?" Paul asked.

Wayne took a newspaper clipping out of his pocket. "Here, you read it."

Paul quickly glanced at the advertisement. It told of a "prestigious, historical landmark for sale, in the heart of Times Square. For seventy years this building, designed by the world-famous architect, Stanford White, has housed 'The Lamb's Club,' America's oldest theatrical club. A bankruptcy forces sale of a property appraised at $1.7 million."

Paul tossed the clipping back to Wayne. "That's funny."

"No, Paul, I'm serious," Wayne replied soberly. "You've got to see it to believe it. It's *exactly* what we need."

"Wayne, it's one thing to trust God for the best, but quite another to be realistic. This is out of the question! We have fifty-five members, with a few over one hundred attending on Sunday. Our annual budget is $65,000. We have $25 in the bank, are praying God will bring in next week's payroll, and you're talking about a million-dollar building. It's absurd!" Paul said sharply.

"Please, Paul. Come and look at it. It can be bought for a fourth of it's appraised value," Wayne argued.

"No . . . I don't want to waste my time going there."

"But aren't you the one who's always told us to let God the Holy Spirit dream great thoughts through us—to ask God to do the impossible—so there is no way we can claim the credit or glory?"

"Yes, but . . ."

"Just come and look at it. If you still feel the same way, I won't bring it up again," Wayne said.

It took several days of coercing to get Paul to accompany a real estate agent to The Lamb's Club.

As they walked under the canopy in front of the big six-story Lamb's Club building at 130 West Forty-fourth Street, Paul had a strange sensation of calmness surround him. The canvas canopy did not more than keep the January rain off them as they waited to unlock the building, but beyond that, perhaps symbolically, there was a mystical sense of what? *Peace? Shelter?* Paul couldn't define it. Nor was his conscious mind even thinking about it.

The real estate agent, a quietly aggressive, middle-aged balding man, was not yet used to his new clients. Most religious groups were fleeing the city. He could not understand why one wanted to stay. Nor could he see how the building would make a good church. True, it did have a beautiful stage and auditorium. And those were the qualities he emphasised in his sales presentation.

"Look at these beautiful oak-panelled walls and plush opera seats," he extolled. "Any congregation would feel very . . . uh . . . religious . . . here. This would make a terrific church sanctuary."

"Yes," Wayne replied, "but we'd use it for plays and concerts, too—as a theater, just as it was designed. And, Paul, you ought to see the restaurant downstairs! It's a carbon copy of the Buckingham Palace grill room!"

The man wrinkled his forehead and wondered what kind of a church group these people represented. A *theater?* A *palace grill room?*

As they walked through the building, Paul began to see why Wayne was excited. It had facilities for every conceivable church ministry and function, both now and in the future. The building needed redecorating and some modernization, but it was structurally sound. To design and replace the Lamb's building would cost several million dollars. The $1.7 million appraisal was modest. The building housed a restaurant with full kitchen facilities, a library, and a five-hundred-seat theater complete with dramatic stage, curtains, and lighting. It had—in addition to the grand ballroom, lounges, and expansive office space—fifty residence rooms.

Paul also saw at once why Wayne sensed the leading of God concerning the Lamb's building. Paul turned to the real estate agent before they left. "Thank you for showing us through. We're definitely interested, but . . ."

"Yes, I know it's a lot of money. Take it to your church board and discuss it. I know the mortgage is around a half million. Maybe I can take an offer for that in to the bank that is handling the bankruptcy.

"Well, you need to know we have absolutely no money for this. We're going to do a feasibility study and ask God if it's His will for us to have the Lamb's."

"Ask God?" the man said, "Oh, you mean *pray.* Yes, Reverend, good. It's a good idea to pray."

For six weeks the Manhattan Church leaders prayed and planned. Joel Tucciarone joined with Mark Weimer, Wayne Rogers, and Paul in developing a feasibility study. A quick check with the realtor showed the building still had not been sold.

The four men went to the Lamb's many times between January and March. They measured and discussed. They prayed and put together their preliminary plan. They refined that plan through long around-the-clock sessions into a seventy-five page proposal to the church board.

Since the Manhattan Church was newly-chartered, and technically a mission project of the denomination, its governing board was made up of men from the denomination. A local board without actual authority handled spiritual matters in the church. All business matters had to go through the denominational channels.

Paul knew he had to do his homework. First, his superiors at the denomination had to be sold on the basic idea. Then they had to be shown how it would work. Paul and his associates saw a plan emerge that *would* be feasible.

"But it is only possible with God's help," Paul explained to Reverend Scutt. "I know the thing sounds crazy—impossible. I was saying the same thing two months ago. But we believe God wants us to have the Lamb's. If God isn't in it, we won't get anywhere with the project because we need to raise nearly $90,000 for the down payment. And humanly speaking, Reverend Scutt, that's impossible. We're going for a miracle!"

Reverend Scutt nodded. "But, how will you pay for it—that's the crucial question—even assuming that God is in it."

"It's all in this feasibility study and proposal," Paul explained. "If we can raise option money and a down payment, we'll put on a city-wide telethon this fall to raise the rest of the money."

"A telethon."

"Yes, like they do for Muscular Dystrophy and Easter Seals. I believe the people of New York would want to help reclaim and redeem Times Square."

"But you haven't had any experience with telethons," Paul's superior reminded him.

"I know. We'll hire an expert to come in and help us pull it off."

"Do you have someone in mind?"

"Yes. Bill Bray has done this kind of thing in other cities, including Chicago. He's offered to help us," Paul answered.

Reverend Scutt shook his head skeptically. "I don't know. Maybe it'll work. In any event I'll send your proposal up to headquarters, and we'll see what happens."

ᔕᔕᔕᔕᔕᔕᔕᔕᔕᔕᔕᔕ

Through negotiations with the bank, Paul had been able to lower the price for the Lamb's considerably. He had offered $450,000 for the bankrupt property. The lender was now responding with a counter offer.

"There is a $475,000 mortgage on the building. We won't sell for less than that, including twenty per cent down," the banker told Paul. "But I'll tell you what. If you'll raise ten per cent as the down payment, we'll hold the property until a new mortgage is written."

Paul gave them a check for $10,000 as earnest money, which denomination leaders had provided as proof of their faith in the project.

"I don't know where the other $37,500 will come from, but we'll get it with God's help," Paul announced.

The lender cleared his throat and mumbled, "That's fine, Reverend. I just hope the Almighty comes through for you on schedule. He only has thirty days until the down payment option money has to be paid, or you'll lose your earnest money deposit and the option to buy the Lamb's."

ᔕᔕᔕᔕᔕᔕᔕᔕᔕᔕᔕᔕ

Exactly one week later, Paul flew to Portsmouth, Virginia. He had been invited to appear on the *700 Club*, produced by the Christian Broadcasting Network. He had planned to show slides of the New York work and tell about some of the exciting ministries of the Manhattan Church of the Nazarene. Included were some slides of the Lamb's building. Paul said to host Pat Robertson, "Here's the dream we're dreaming, Pat." Then he told of the "impossibility," humanly speaking, of ever seeing that dream realized. "But we've already come so far in the beginning of our dream that we can't help but trust God," Paul said. Paul told how the Hari Krishna cult had come along immediately after the offer of Manhattan Church had been accepted. Even though the cult had offered more money, the lending institution was obligated to proceed with Paul's group. "We have about three weeks to raise the down payment or the building will be sold to the Hari Krishna group," Paul said quietly.

Pat leaned across the desk and reached for Paul's hand. "Brother, I'm going to pray for you right now!" Pat, his co-host, and Paul joined hands as Pat led in prayer for Paul and the success of the Lamb's project in New York.

As the program ended and the men walked out of the glare of the TV lights to the edge of the big *700 Club* set, Pat turned to Paul and shook hands. He leaned in and said quietly, "I'll stand by you in this. Put me down for fifteen."

Paul barely had time to reply, "Thanks very much," and Pat was gone. Paul turned to Pat's associate. "I'm sure Pat didn't mean fifteen dollars, he meant fifteen-*hundred,* right?" he asked the co-host.

The associate said, "I think he meant fifteen thousand."

⮑⮑⮑⮑⮑⮑⮑⮑⮑⮑⮑

A check for $15,000 from Pat Robertson came within the next two weeks. A few smaller gifts had come in also, but another $15,000 was needed only days before the deadline.

An officer of the Tremont Savings and Loan Association of the Bronx (the lending institution that held the mortgage) called to ask about Paul's progress in raising the money.

"We'll make it, I'm sure," Paul answered.

"M-mm . . . I see. Well, I just wanted to see how you were doing in your fund raising. You know, of course, that we cannot give you any additional time."

"Yes, I know," Paul answered.

"Well, we'll be looking for you at the end of the month. If not . . . well, we have another offer. The Hari Krishna group also wants the building. They have their checkbook ready. So, if you can't put the deal together. . ."

"We'll be there?" Paul replied sharply.

But his last hope was for help from the community itself. He got an appointment with Gerald Schoenfeld, president of the Shubert Foundation, an organization synonomous with Broadway and Times Square. Schoenfeld read over the proposal and asked a few questions concerning the Manhattan Church of the Nazarene and plans for theatrical and musical productions.

Paul told him of their dreams for a Christian renaissance in the arts and their desire to exert a positive influence in the neighborhood. "We'd like to have a small part in cleaning up Times Square, Mr. Schoenfeld," Paul told him. "We'd rather see an organization like ours go into that building than more massage parlors, sex shops, or drug dealers. We feel we have something positive and constructive to contribute to the neighborhood, sir."

"Well, those are noble objectives. And we *would* like to clean up Times Square . . ." Schoenfeld agreed.

"And, we feel our purposes in theater and music are more in keeping with the history of the Lamb's than are those of the other group that wants to buy the building," Paul added.

"What other group? Someone else wants to buy the Lamb's?"

"Yes, sir. The Hari Krishna Society."

Schoenfeld winced. His only knowledge of the group was through seeing the members attract public attention with their long robes, shaved heads, and strange chants and dancing.

"How much do you need, Reverend?"

"We need $15,000 by Monday."

"You've go it. Stop by my office first thing Monday morning and I'll give you a check. I'll have my car take you to the lawyer's for the closing," Schoenfeld told him.

The Manhattan Church paid $47,500 to the Tremont Savings and Loan Association on the last day of its option, only hours before the deadline. The papers were signed and the church now had thirty days to raise an additional $75,000, the remainder of the down payment and money needed for repairs and operating expenses required by the lender. Meanwhile, the church could occupy the Lamb's building and begin renovations. A major fund-raising effort was launched and intensified. Church members emptied their small savings accounts, borrowed from friends and relatives, and called on others to help. But it was obvious by July 1 that they were going to fall significantly short by some $57,000. The lender, however, agreed this time to a fifteen-day extension. By July 15, the funds were still $30,000 short of the goal. Again an extension was granted but this time only six short days. As the July 21 final deadline approached, it appeared the church would lose its option to buy the Lamb's and forfeit its initial down payment, because they lacked $30,000 with no hope of even coming close.

Once again, however, the small group cried out to God. Once more they would ask the impossible and trust.

Before the final deadline, the Church of the Nazarene, through its Department of Home Missions, agreed to provide the final amount—with only five hours to spare!

Tearfully, joyfully, the congregation celebrated the contract signing, and the Lamb's became the new home of the Manhattan Church of the Nazarene. The congregation was happy too for the denomination's commitment to urban missions.

IV. The Exciting Church

Thirty-three

THE LAMB'S BUILDING was not immediately transformed, but by summer most of the painting and renovations had been completed. Everyone was quite relieved to at last
have a permanent church home.

Michael Christensen, who had spent a year and a summer as
intern when the church work first began, now considered drop-
ping out of college for another full year of service at the Lamb's.
He had become involved in nearly every aspect of the ministry
and was especially gifted in the development of public relations
pieces, brochures, newsletters, and prayer support letters. Paul
had asked Mike to serve as director of publications, and after
prayerful consideration, he accepted.

He set up an area for himself in the old library of the six-story
Lamb's building. The character and charm of the big oak-
paneled room usually inspired his creativity. But this afternoon,
one of those steamy summer New York days, the room was
uncomfortable without air conditioning.

Mike decided to go for a walk and perhaps take some pictures
for the next newsletter. It was almost dusk and he could come
back in an hour or two when the room would be cooler.

Walking the streets was not much more comfortable. The
exhaust from the cars gave off not only more of the unwanted
heat but noxious fumes as well. The pollution stung his eyes and
nose, and he blinked several times. Acrid smells of rotting garbage drifted from a nearby alley, and Mike hurried away from
the stench.

In some of the windows along the street he was subjected to a
more subtle kind of pollution, the kind that smudges the mind

and imagination. "Live Nude Dancing" declared one sign. Across the street a theater marquee boasted of "kinky sex experiences never before imagined," and posters showed nude women masturbating with snakes and caressing dogs and donkeys. Other posters depicted homosexual couples and groups.

Mike walked past a place called The New Meeting Room, one of the dozens of new massage parlors in or around Times Square. Two sailors were talking to a man standing on the sidewalk handing out flyers. Suddenly, the three of them laughed at some joke and the sailors hurried inside.

A few doors away Mike passed another massage parlor. Three women in their early twenties sat or stood around lazily. Two of them were wearing bikinis, a third, wearing only a bra and panties and smoking a long cigarette, stared back at him.

As Mike walked on for several blocks it seemed to him that the Manhattan Church had quite a mission field in its own front yard. It was getting dark now and the street lights were coming on. Under one of the lamps across the street, a prostitute was at her "station" where men in cars cruising past could see her and stop without difficulty. Mike watched as two black men approached her. He noticed they were not "johns" (customers). He figured them to be pimps or drug pushers. As he got closer, Mike could tell they were arguing about something. One man grabbed the woman while the other tried to take her purse. The woman yelled loudly.

"Get outta here, you creeps! Leave me alone!"

The taller of the two men swung viciously and hit the woman in the face. She screamed but continued to struggle. The tall man hit her again, and again.

Mike froze for an instant. If he didn't do something, they would likely beat the woman to death. Mike could already see blood on her face and terror in her eyes. Her screams had turned to frightened whimpering and pleading. But the tall man did not stop.

Mike ran toward them with an idea. He took his camera and pointed it in the direction of the struggle.

"Hey!" Mike yelled, just as the flash went off and blinded them momentarily. The two men looked dumbly at Mike. Mike snapped again with the flash unit. The men reacted this time. Preferring to protect their anonymity to whatever they wanted in the woman's purse, the two men let go of her and started after Mike.

In a way this is what he had wanted, but he had also feared that it might happen. Mike took off as fast as he could, the two men in pursuit. The smaller man almost caught up with him, but his endurance was short-lived. Mike avoided the temptation of darting down a dark alley to try to lose his pursuers—that might be going from bad to worse.

As the short man became winded and fell behind, the taller man gained. Mike was gasping for breath himself. Although several people watched the chase, no one attempted to stop it or intervene. The best help Mike could hope for was to have people on the sidewalk move aside as he ran by.

Mike turned a corner and glanced over his shoulder. Thirty feet behind him was the tall man in determined pursuit. Looking back was a mistake. Mike's shoe caught on something jutting out of the sidewalk and he sprawled on the pavement. Somehow he recovered his balance even as he fell and was up again just as the tall man got to him. He heard and felt his shirt tearing and shuddered to think how close he'd come to getting caught.

Mike ran even faster, his heart pumping madly in the summer heat. From somewhere came new strength and he began to increase his lead in the chase. Soon there was a half a block between them, then a block. After running several more blocks, turning up one street and down another, Mike finally lost his pursuer and would-be assailant.

In the early months, of the Manhattan Church ministry, personal evangelism had held a high priority. Of late this fervor had diminished, but one of the church's couples made a new commitment to evangelism and taught the Campus Crusade "Wit-

nessing as a Way of Life" Evangelism Training Course. The
concepts presented in the course nearly revolutionized the
evangelistic efforts of the Manhattan Church.

One Saturday following the training course, Mark Weimer
and Jim Hullinger left the Lamb's building for "witnessing training."

Just past the public library was Bryant Park. In August the
park was always filled with people. Mark and Jim looked for one
person whom they might approach and share the gospel.

"Over there," Jim pointed. "That old man on the park bench."
Mark nodded and the two walked toward the man. He was in his
late seventies, they guessed, and looked lost and lonely.

The old man introduced himself as John O'Shaughnessey and
there was a trace of Irish brogue in his speech.

After a few exchanged pleasantries, John told the men he
was seventy-eight years old. He listened to their remarks and
responded politely. He didn't volunteer much background
information, so Mark tried to get more. When it seemed
he could trust the two young men, John told them his bizarre
story.

"M' father came over here from Ireland. He was a bartender
and worked hard. I was the youngest of m' brothers and sisters,"
John explained.

"Where do you live?" Mark asked.

"Here," John replied simply.

"No, I mean where in New York?"

"Here. I live here . . . in the park."

The two young men looked at each other in disbelief. "But
how, why?"

John explained that he had been an inmate in a New York
mental institution since suffering a nervous breakdown some
forty years earlier. He had been there through World War II,
the fifties and the Korean War; he was inside all during the
sixties and Viet Nam, and only now was on the outside.

"But what about your family; how did you get out?" Mark
asked.

"I think my family died," John said sadly. "I'm not sure." He
explained that he had been confined so long that they often

neglected to lock his door. He had never given the institution any trouble, so they trusted him.

"But one day," John smiled, "I decided to leave. I wanted to visit my sister. I had never been out in the forty years they kept me. But now I wanted to see my sister. I had some money and found a subway train and took it to Sixth Avenue and Fortieth Street. But my sister's house was gone. And so was she," John said sadly.

"Then what did you do?" Mark asked.

"Well, I had no money, and I was too old to get a job. I suppose I should have gone back to the asylum, but I couldn't. I didn't want to die there. They think everyone there is crazy. Some are, I suppose. But I'm not crazy."

Mark shook his head. "How do you eat? Where do you sleep?"

John's eyes sparkled. "There's a boy, he works at a place called Burger King. Every day he brings me stuff they are supposed to throw away; but it's good, not garbage. And I sleep here, on the bench. When it rains I find some place else."

"That's absolutely incredible!" Mark exclaimed. "John, I want you to come with us. We'd like to be your friends. We have a building called the Lamb's, and we have extra rooms and food there."

"Oh, no thank you. I can't take charity."

Mark thought for a moment. "Okay, then how about if we give you a job?"

"A job? What could I do?"

"Well, we need a part-time janitor. You could dump trash, sweep, and clean up. We'll give you free room and board—and pay you besides. We'll help you get back on your feet."

Mark and Jim talked the next day with the authorities. They learned that John had no serious mental problems and had been confined all those years because no one cared enough to look into his case. The authorities officially released "Poppa John," as he was nicknamed by a loving staff and congregation, into the custody of the Manhattan Church. Jim helped John file for Social Security and opened a checking and savings account for him. At age seventy-eight, John O'Shaughnessey was at last "*somebody*."

"Poppa John" came to church on Sunday with the younger people of the congregation. After a few weeks he prayed to receive Christ and began an entirely new chapter in his life.

∽∾∽∾∽∾∽∾∽∾∽∾∽∾∽

Joyce had spent thirteen months in the Walter Hoving Home for Girls. The understanding, love, and acceptance they showed her there was exactly what she needed. Soon after her arrival Joyce accepted Christ.

For a little over a year she was given help and counsel in changing over twenty years of habits, beliefs, and psychological scars.

It wasn't easy. Each of the hundreds of men Joyce had encountered as a prostitute had left her with another layer of hatred wrapped around her mind and personality. Her shell was hardened and had to be chisled away patiently.

But by last Christmas, Joyce had become a new person—clean, healthy, and on her way to emotional recovery. Her faith had likewise been nourished, and now Joyce was walking daily with God.

After a brief stay at home with her parents, it was obvious she had to move out. While her folks were grateful Joyce had been cured of her drug problem, they didn't appreciate her new religious "fanaticism." It seemed to them that she was always preaching and trying to convert them. In her excitement and joy after finding the answers to her own problems, Joyce didn't realize that she was being too zealous.

To help keep peace, she decided to move into a New York City apartment, since her folks lived in the suburbs.

She checked with the people at the Walter Hoving Home for Girls for advice. They encouraged her to get into a Christian environment where she could serve Christ.

They gave her the name and address of the Lamb's and suggested she apply there for a volunteer staff position and residency.

Joyce moved into the Lamb's and immediately found ways to use her talents in counselling other girls, witnessing, and organizing. She proved so capable that she was given the responsibility of "dorm mother" for the girls in residence at the Lamb's.

Thirty-four

BY OCTOBER, 1975, the Lamb's was becoming known as a sanctuary for the "lost sheep" of Times Square. The media had picked up on the idea of a church in midtown Manhattan that was striving to reach the socialite as well as the prostitute; that was ministering to the upward-striving affluent businessman and career woman as well as to the derelicts and elderly poor. Slowly, church attendance began to increase.

But one thing angered Paul Moore as he stood in his third floor office. Every time he looked out his window, he was confronted with a view of the Hudson Theater, one of the best-known porno movie houses in Times Square. The theater featured films showing crude sex acts between men and women, as well as homosexual acts and bestiality.

Paul had thought about standing in front of the theater with a videotape camera and recording pictures of who went in and out. Later these tapes could be replayed on the public access cable TV channel.

He thought about picketing and disrupting the theater, harassing it with threats of TV and newspaper publicity—of even tearing the place apart.

However, God seemed to say to Paul, no. *That's not My way. Offer them an alternative.*

Paul took Mark Weimer with him to visit the theater manager. Paul expected to see a seedy, sinister man—the classic pervert— in the office. Instead, the manager was a middle-aged man who could have been an insurance salesman, hardware dealer, or auto repairman.

Paul introduced himself and told about their occupancy of the Lamb's building. "I've come to you with an olive branch in one hand and a club in the other," he said. Then he launched into a brief but fiery sermon about the evils of appealing to men's baser instincts and leading kids astray.

"You can plead innocence or ignorance, but you are part of the demonic forces out to destroy men's souls!" Paul charged. "And I won't stop until we close down the filth!"

"You're wasting your time, Reverend," the manager smirked. "If I close down, there'll be another porno movie house open tomorrow. Look, you can't tell other people what's for them. Now, I agree with you myself. This stuff *is* filth. These creeps come in here and masturbate or worse while the picture's on. But so what? It's a free country. It's not my thing—I think the whole thing is disgusting. But everyone has to make a living. To each his own, I say," the man shrugged.

"So now you justify it on the basis of good ol' American free enterprise?" Paul snapped. "Well, maybe *you* can turn your head away when those men come in here and make Sodom and Gomorrah look like a Disney film by comparison. But we can't tolerate it any longer. We came to *demand* that you change!"

The manager shook his head. "We even tried Disney; but we went broke. Nope. We'll have to stick with adult films, Reverend. Sorry."

"No . . . you're not sorry. I'll tell you what *sorry* is! We'll call the press and TV people. We'll picket this place day and night. We'll take videotape pictures of your customers and show 'em to all New York! I'm going to find out who owns this building. And we'll rent buses and be on their manicured front lawns in the suburbs. We'll call in the press and TV and tell the whole world. Now *that's* sorry, mister!"

The manager was beginning to fidget and his face looked pinched, drawn.

Paul continued, "And if I find that a company with stockholders owns this building, we'll storm their stockholders' meeting and ask them what they think about little boys and girls having to confront this garbage on their way to Sunday school across the street!"

The manager waved his arm, "All right, all right. I get the picture. What do you want?"

Paul smiled, suddenly caught off guard. He hadn't expected such a sudden victory. He thought for a moment. "We want you to get rid of the filth, that's all. You *could* go one better, though. The Billy Graham organization has a brand new film called *The Hiding Place*. It's about the Holocaust and should do well in New York. You've been running garbage until now. Why don't you clean up and redeem this place by showing *The Hiding Place*?"

"I'll see what I can do," the man said grimly.

~~~~~~~~~~~~~~~~~~~~

Paul investigated and learned that the Hudson Theater was owned by a major steel company's foundation. Paul contacted them. "Look," he explained, "maybe you don't know this, but you ought to look into it." He then repeated his demands, keeping his voice as friendly and businesslike as possible. "I know you'll want to check it out. I'd hate to have to write letters to your constituents and alert the press."

Reaction was swift and definite. The Hudson Theater was immediately closed. The foundation spent $150,000 to clean, repair, renovate, and remodel the building. They recovered the soiled and stained seats, replaced the carpeting, and painted all the walls and woodwork. Finally, a brand new marquee announced:

New York Premier
HIDING PLACE

The World Wide Pictures' film played to standing-room-only crowds for five weeks. The sidewalks were crowded with people, many of them of obvious Jewish heritage with their beards, skull caps, and prayer shawls. Paul watched with growing satisfaction and praise for God. It was a genuine miracle. One of the most disgusting places in Manhattan had been "redeemed" and was now a tangible witness to God's greatness. Paul knew now that Satan *could* be defeated, even in his own backyard. With new zest Paul felt ready to take on the next great task.

Thirty-five

THE MANHATTAN CHURCH was now a permanent and visible part of the neighborhood. Its ministries began to blossom and expand, and there seemed to be no limit to the enthusiasm of the members.

But Paul had never taken the Lamb's building for granted. It was now October and the mortgage and escrow payments began on schedule. For several months since the closing of the deal, Paul had been working with Bill Bray, Mark Weimer, and others in planning the city-wide telethon. Paul insisted that they do their homework on the project. If successful, it would relieve them of much of the financial pressures of the building.

Bill was the coordinator and Mark was the producer. They brought their strategy to Paul for review. "We'll contact 4,000 churches about the TV special, send out 420,000 handbills, 110,000 brochures, 50,000 buttons, 10,000 posters, 7,000 newsletters, and 6,000 postcards. We have ads in 31 newspapers and magazines—including *TV Guide*—and promotional material has been sent to over 1,000 churches requesting it. We plan to generate media coverage through press conferences, news releases, interviews, and luncheons. We'll be getting appearances from Graham Kerr (The Galloping Gourmet), Pat Boone, Tom Skinner, and CBN's Pat Robertson—all of whom will tape radio and TV spots to alert viewers of the "I Care TV Special." We'll have nearly 400 telephones in 6 centers across New York, with 1,000 counsellors recruited from evangelical churches," Bray reported.

Paul was impressed with their thoroughness and expectations. As he went over their plans and they showed him how the promotion, production, and follow-up would be handled, he got excited. "Men, I'm convinced that the "I Care TV Special" on October 26 is going to be the boldest religious telethon ever to hit New York!"

WPIX-TV, channel 11, had reserved five hours of prime TV time, from 8:00 P.M. to 1:00 A.M., so the Manhattan Church of the Nazarene could reach an amazing number of people. The church had twin objectives. Not only were they eager to raise financial support for the Lamb's, but Paul wanted the "I Care TV Special" to demonstrate God's concern as well.

"It will be an unprecedented opportunity to present the gospel to millions of people who normally wouldn't listen. Let's try to reach these people for Jesus," he said.

Finally, the six weeks of intensive planning and preparation ended. Four giant TV production vans parked at the curb ouside the Lamb's. The fifteen-man technical crew began to carry in heavy lights, cables, cameras, and related gear.

Choirs and music groups rehearsed in various parts of the building while the finishing paint touch-ups were made to the set. The auditorium had been transformed into a professional television studio. Counsellors began to arrive and take position at the banks of telephones set up in the restaurant. The grand ballroom was now a mail room and record-keeping and resting area.

Director Roger Lounsbury went over last minute details with Paul and the TV crew as the twenty-one piece orchestra tuned up.

As eight o'clock drew closer, some of the TV crew grew a bit testy as they rushed to be ready in time. John Hillyer, a member of Manhattan Church and an NBC cameraman, was pressed into duty as assistant director when the person assigned to the job failed to show up.

John went right to work. "That audio man is out to sabotage us!" he complained to the producer. "He hasn't checked any of the lines, and we're almost ready to go on the air."

The producer went off to look for the technical director and audio man, leaving John to utter a prayer. "Lord, please rescue us. This production could really be a mess. I pray You'll help us with all the details. These secular TV guys aren't concerned about what we look like or if the sound is working right, but *we* do—we don't want this to be an embarrassment to You," he prayed.

Somehow, miraculously perhaps, it all came together. There were hundreds of calls that came in to pledge support for the Lamb's and other Manhattan Church ministries. There were hundreds of others from those who called for spiritual help or to receive Christ, including a prostitute, some teenagers, a man dying in a hospital, and others.

The telethon, in addition to special guest appearances, featured film clips, street interviews, testimonies, commentary, and music by Christian artists.

The leadership of Paul's denomination was also well represented. District Superintendent Scutt observed near the end of the telethon that he was pleased with the results. "We believe God has a definite ministry here in Manhattan, and He is proving it through this television program," Reverend Scutt said.

General Superintendent Eugene Stowe and other leaders from the Nazarene church were present to reaffirm their prayers and personal financial support. Stowe reminded the television audience, "This church cares, as Christ cared, and we are part of that church . . . with love and caring for the city of New York."

By the time the telethon signed off the air, some *four* thousand viewers had phoned in pledges totalling $320,000.

Paul thanked everyone as they left, loosened his tie, took off his jacket, and sat down on one of the auditorium seats while TV crewmen noisily began to take down the equipment. He breathed a long and quiet prayer of gratefulness and reflected on their "dare-saintedness." A little over one hundred people—from a church less than two years old—talked to millions for five hours and blanketed the city, as well as the entire New York metro area, with the gospel of Jesus Christ. This was truly a work of God.

Thirty-six

JOE COLAIZZI LOOKED at the face in the mirror as he shaved. A happy, peaceful person looked back. Was it possible that one man could have changed so much in the time since he had left Pittsburgh for Santa Fe and returned? Even Dolly's family had noticed the change. Although he worked for his former brother-in-law, Joe, he lived with Ron, another of Dolly's brothers. Ron had been fascinated by Joe's account of his conversion to Christianity and the new life Joe now had with Christ living in him. It wasn't long before Ron had expressed his desire to become a believer.

Ron and Joe both were soon praying that Dolly and the rest of the family would come to Christ. Either because of or in spite of Joe's simplistic faith and witness, Dolly did decide to become a Christian.

With Dolly it wasn't simply a matter of a simple, quick decision. Very deep and considered repentance preceded her commitment. Dolly prayed with Joe, then went through her apartment and gathered up all her astrology books, horoscope charts, and occult materials. After these were all burned, she came, weeping, to receive Jesus Christ. A glorious and exciting conversion experience followed.

With Dolly and Ron now dedicated Christians, her family became even closer than before. Often Joe would invite them to church on Sundays.

Joe finished the remodeling project for Dolly's brothers and went into business for himself, doing odd jobs and carpentry—all the while wondering what new venture God was preparing for him.

While in church each Sunday, still a "babe in Christ," Joe practiced a simple, almost mystical faith in God. He listened to each sermon and Bible reading to learn what God might be saying to him.

This week a guest preacher was in the pulpit—Moishe Rosen—a Hebrew-Christian who embraced Jesus Christ as the Messiah and Christianity as an extension of Judaism. Rosen told the Youngstown congregation about the missionary work of the organization he had founded, Jews for Jesus, in New York City.

"In New York," Rosen told them, "you can witness to literally *thousands* of people in just a few hours. We give out tracts or preach on street corners to hundreds at a time!"

The concept of sharing Christ with so many in need appealed to Joe. He was reminded of Rosen's illustration from the life of the Old Testament patriarch, Abraham. "Abraham responded to God's call with a very special Hebrew word. In English it translates as 'Lord, here am I.' But in the Hebrew, the word implies deep, thoughtful, and prayerful commitment. It isn't a word to be used in casual conversation or treated lightly. It is to be used carefully and reverently. 'Lord, here am I,' " Rosen told them.

Joe turned the phrase over and over in his mind. Was God calling him to New York? How could he be sure?

"Lord," Joe prayed, "I don't know if You want me to go to New York. But You know my heart. You know my desire to serve You. If You want me in New York or Pittsburgh or South America or anywhere, I just want to say, I'm available. 'Lord, here am I.' "

⁓⁓⁓⁓⁓⁓⁓⁓⁓⁓⁓⁓

Barbara Billings, a charter member of Manhattan Church, had likewise come a long way in her faith and Christian experience. She had learned to study the Bible and pray. A void was filled in her life as she saw how God worked not only in her life and experience, but, sometimes, *through* her in touching others as well.

Cheryl, Cari, and Todd were three such examples, God had touched their lives, it was certain. But what if she had never taken the job at Mr. Lee's, or what if she had never shared her faith in conversations and friendship with them. They might never have become Christians and started their own chains of witness, both at Mr. Lee's to co-workers and to others.

Barbara smiled at the providence of God, and how He cares for every detail in His own way and time. For example, there was that new man in her life. Joseph Bruccoleri, born in Sicily, had come to America as a child. When he had come to New York from California, he had started attending services at the Lamb's because a friend on the West Coast had told him of the work. It was here he had met and dated Barbara. Joseph was a new Christian, but he was growing and maturing quickly. He was eager to learn the truths that had radically altered his life.

Barbara enjoyed their dates. They had so many compatibilities that their times together were always rich, exciting, and fun experiences. But as she dated the handsome dark-haired Joseph, many of her old doubts returned to nag and confuse her. She had never had the commitment required for a lasting relationship with a man. Her old philosophy had been to find fulfillment in herself. Now she sought happiness and peace of mind in Christ.

Joseph proposed to her, but she wasn't sure what she should do.

"Why do you wonder?" Joseph asked her. "I love you and you love me. We enjoy being together . . . we have much in common, such as our love for the Lord. I believe that He has kept us both single so that we would find each other."

"I wonder if I've grown enough," Barbara confessed. "Before I met you, before I was a Christian, I ran from place to place, from job to job—always dissatisfied. How do I know I've outgrown those old habits?"

"I can't believe you were ever like that," Joseph said, smiling. "I've always seen a confident, organized, and stable person.

And, as I said, I believe God has ordained our relationship. Now, I want to marry you."

Barbara nodded. "I've been praying about it since you first asked me two months ago. God has given me the assurance that it's His will that we marry. I now see that I can marry you out of a desire to give, not out of some need of mine."

Joseph did not answer with words. Instead, he took her in his arms and kissed her with all his love.

Thirty-seven

FEW METROPOLITAN DISTRICTS in the world have such contrasting extremes as Times Square. The Lamb's is sandwiched between the sleazy massage parlor-houses of prostitution of Forty-second Street at one end, and the elegant, sophisticated Broadway theaters of Shubert Alley at the opposite end. Between these two extremes lie just about every kind of business and individual imaginable. This presence of so many facets of life is what both fascinates and repels.

Because of the hookers, pimps, drug pushers, and sex and porno merchants, there is an *evil* presence that permeates like a low-level fog. A person cannot escape this presence in New York. Yet, this is only the *obvious* evil, the tip of the iceberg. In Manhattan, there are *organized* evil factors that add to this high concentration of evil power: Mafia and street gangs, crooked politicians and businesses, the abuse of power on every level, hedonism and self-centered glamour are everywhere. The people flaunt their antisocial and anti-Christian attitudes and lifestyles. One out of every four males between eighteen and thirty-four in Manhattan is a homosexual.

Not only was it proving difficult to have a Christian church in Times Square, it was hard just coping with the concentration of evil powers and presences. The skirmishes were always fought on an individual level, so the casualties were more crippling to the church. The battles were emotional, physical, and spiritual. Many believers, especially new Christians, were not equipped to handle the intensity of the evil influences. The stresses and pressures of living a Christian lifestyle and having a godly influence in work or social circles was difficult at best. Many outsiders—people coming to Manhattan from Ohio, Indiana, and even California—could not always cope. It seemed to Paul as soon as interns or staff people were trained and effective, they "burned out" from the stress and pressures. Soon they left.

It was a constant struggle to find and use qualified people in the outreaches of the church.

While Paul and the Christians at the Lamb's were contending with the evil powers over Manhattan, on occasion Paul found himself struggling with relationships within his own denomination.

Questions by outsiders concerning the Manhattan Church tended to be primarily about methods and styles; doctrinal differences were minimal and inconsequential.

The Lamb's had received wide attention in the denomination. As a result pastors and leaders never knew what to expect. There was much about New York and its lifestyles, influences, attitudes, and habits that they could never really understand. This fact only increased misunderstanding. Many from the denomination never understood Paul's approach to the city nor his style, which they frequently criticized as "too worldly," "flippant," or "casual." They pointed to other Nazarene congregations that they considered to be "real churches" and urged Paul to pattern his urban work after their suburban models.

Yet, when traditional Nazarenes came to New York and visited the church, they were surprised to discover that the services were "authentic" and in the old-fashioned church tradition, filled with warmth, enthusiasm, fervent preaching, sound teaching, and plenty of appropriately placed "amens" from the congregation. It seemed to these visitors that revival was the norm at Manhattan Church.

Visitors at services from other Nazarene churches would often comment on how they had been blessed and had misjudged the church and Paul's ministry.

But these misunderstandings ("hassles," as Paul called them) continued. Sometimes they were serious, some seemed superficial. For example, there was the problem of people appearing on the TV special who were Pentecostal or Charismatic. Some felt this would cause the Nazarenes themselves to be identified with these groups and their doctrines, thus losing their own denominational distinctives.

Another problem was that the TV special was so widely viewed that people were solicited to donate to the Lamb's from Pennsylvania, New York, New Jersey, and New England—some donors were members of *other* Nazarene churches.

A third question asked was, "How can we spend so much each year ($300,000 plus) to maintain a work of this magnitude in one location when so many churches have been working so long and hard with virtually little help from the denomination?"

But no matter how constricted Paul might have felt or how frustrated the Nazarene authorities might have been at Paul's methods, the two believed in each other and never "gave up."

Perhaps one man was responsible more than anyone else for being able to smooth the waters. Ron Mercer, successful businessman and lay leader in the denomination, became Paul's advocate in Kansas City.

Ron, as a vice-president of the Xerox Corporation and president of the Xerox East division, demonstrated a high level of ability both with his firm and in his denomination. He had recently been relocated by Xerox from their offices in the Chicago suburb of Naperville. When he moved to Connecticut to head the Xerox East operation, Ron and his wife, Yvonne, drove down to New York on Sundays to attend services at the Lamb's. They became members of the Manhattan Church, and Ron started an adult Sunday school class.

Ron and Yvonne became deeply involved in the Lamb's

projects and with its people. They offered their Connecticut home as a retreat house for church planning sessions, and they offered themselves for service in the church.

On more than one occasion Ron went to New York district headquarters or the national headquarters in Kansas City to intercede on Paul's behalf. "Look, Paul Moore is all right. You see him as different, unorthodox. Well, he is, but he's true to the Lord. He's my pastor, and he's feeding us. Only his methods are unorthodox; his doctrine is orthodox."

Ron often became the interpreter of the New York work and many times cleared up the confusion between the Manhattan Church and the denomination. In the process, he and Yvonne became close personal friends of Paul and Sharon.

❧❧❧❧❧❧❧❧❧❧❧❧❧

Jim Hullinger was working his usual night-shift duty at the L'Marquis Hotel. He chuckled to himself after looking at the names on the guest register. *You'd think people could be more creative,* he mused, seeing that nearly a third of the weekend guests were "Mr. and Mrs. Smith."

Jim yawned and looked at his watch. Eleven thirty—there probably would be little activity between now and when his shift ended. Most people were registered by now.

He was suddenly aware of a man in the lobby. Jim hadn't seen him come in, but the man had moved quickly to the small counter where Jim stood.

"I want all the money," the man snarled. Jim was staring into the barrel of a .38 revolver with the hammer cocked. Jim's army M.P. training told him the man meant business. *If the hammer wasn't cocked, I might try to disarm him by grabbing the gun before he could pull the trigger,* Jim thought.

"Sure, the money's yours," Jim told the gunman. "Just be cool, man." He opened the cash drawer and gave the man the money—about $100 in bills.

The robber pushed his way behind the counter. There was no one else in the lobby, and the man was in a rage.

"This ain't all your money. Open the safe!"

"But I don't know the combination," Jim argued.

The big man slammed Jim to the floor. Again, Jim's military instincts told him he should have tried to protect himself with a disarming tactic before this. On the floor with a potential killer standing over him, he was completely vulnerable.

"You open that safe or you're one dead turkey!" the man threatened.

Jim was thoroughly scared now. He really didn't know the combination. He felt the cold hard metal of the gun jammed in his ear.

Jim's head was flattened against the floor and the man's big boot was crushing his neck.

"I'm gonna count to ten and if you don't open that safe, I'm gonna splatter your brains on this floor," the gunman angrily promised.

"One. . ."

Jim wished he knew the combination.

"Two. . ."

"Please," Jim pleaded, "I can't open it. I don't know how!"

"Three. . .!"

This mindless idiot doesn't care, Jim thought desperately. *He'll pull that trigger and not feel a thing.*

"Four! You ain't got much time, man. Five. . ."

Jim had five seconds to live.

"Six. . ."

So many things were racing through Jim's mind.

"Seven. . ."

Jim was shaking with fear but knew he'd be with God.

"Eight. . ."

Lord, I'm in your hands, he prayed.

"Nine." The inflection in the word had the sound of a final warning. Jim braced for the explosion. When it came, it was different than he had expected. It was painful, but in his neck, not his head. He had heard no gunfire. And he was still alive.

Slowly his senses returned.

He was not bleeding and he had not been shot. The man had stomped on his neck and ran off with the cash drawer receipts without shooting him.

Jim was still shaking when the police came on the scene later to take his report. It seemed that he could still feel the pain of the gun barrel being pushed into his ear.

Then it dawned on him that God had saved his life. Gratefulness and release flooded over him in a way he'd never felt before.

"Oh, thank You, Jesus . . . thank You" he said out loud.

Thirty-eight

B Y MARCH, PAUL and Sharon were physically, mentally, and spiritually tired. The mounting pressures and tensions from their three years had been more than some people experience in a lifetime. Paul and Sharon always took time off for a vacation with their family, but the last retreat for just the two of them had been in the fall of 1972, before their move to Manhattan. That fact, plus the increasing stress in coping with the Lamb's ministry and resulting struggles became too much.

"We've got to get away for a while," Paul told Sharon. She agreed with him thoroughly.

"Sometimes I feel that our lives are going to explode," she said.

"That's sort of what Ron Mercer told me. He said you either *go apart* for rest and refilling of your stamina and creativity, or you *come apart* at the seams," Paul said.

A few days later their plane landed in the Virgin Islands where Paul and Sharon were to have their first personal, extended retreat since moving to New York. There would be no church matters, financial needs, policy problems, or children to distract them. Nor would there be telephones to interrupt and appointments to keep. A boat took them to remote Yost Van Dyke Island in the chain.

Yost Van Dyke Island and Manhattan were as different as paradise and hades.

Paul and Sharon were dropped off by boat at a beautiful villa overlooking a turquoise lagoon. They carried their luggage and boxes of food into the house.

Sharon caught her breath at its beauty, luxury, and solitude. It was like a dream. Tropical birds sang outdoors. The warm sun was brighter than Paul had ever remembered seeing it, especially through the dingy city-scapes of Manhattan.

Paul put his arm around Sharon and drew her to him as they looked out the picture window to the sea. It was so incredibly beautiful that for several moments neither of them spoke.

ᔕᔕᔕᔕᔕᔕᔕᔕᔕᔕᔕ

The warm days and quiet evenings at Yost Van Dyke Island were both refreshing and exciting. As each day passed, Paul and Sharon swam, walked, talked, prayed, read, loved, relaxed, and grew closer than ever before. Sharon had longed for these uninterrupted days of shared intimacy and rest.

They had taken several books, including their Bibles, along on the trip, and although they were together for long hours in sun and shade, they seldom spoke during these times of spiritual and mental refilling.

At home, such extended readings were not possible. For Sharon, the demands on her time as wife and mother left little time for reading and reflection. Her prayer life had become little more than quick pleas for God's help.

Paul's schedule was likewise hectic. True, he did read extensively in his sermon preparation, but he seldom had time to seek out spiritiual insights beyond that. In fact, a friend from the church had given Paul a copy of a book he had wanted his pastor to read. In the continual rush, it was never read. When he heard that Paul and Sharon were going away for a retreat, he brought a second copy to Paul to be read on the island.

This book was small, and Paul had tucked it in the suitcase with several others. It was entitled *"A Master Plan For Evangelism,"* by Robert Coleman. It was to change Paul's life and thinking, and was pivotal in a whole new approach to his ministry.

The principle Coleman presented was simple enough: Jesus Christ spent his life with twelve men and imparted His truth, lifestyle, and disciplines to these twelve men. Then, He sent them out to reproduce themselves and perform the same mission in other lives.

Paul began to think and write down his thoughts and concepts of how this "discipling" method could work in his church.

"I might be better off," he told Sharon as he reflected, "if I could find six men who have a heart for God, are teachable, have a pliable spirit, a will to succeed, and the stability to give at least one year's commitment to this relationship." Leadership training would then be less haphazard and "burn-out" not as frequent.

Paul began a daily journal to record his thoughts and goals. "I'm learning that you measure life by accountability. I need to be a better manager of time," he told Sharon.

The Coleman book revolutionized Paul's thinking regarding evangelism and leadership training, but now God opened his mind to several other exciting concepts and principles.

Under the heading "The Exciting Church," Paul wrote in his journal ideas concerning the ministry and activities of the members of a local church. "There are six areas of involvement in the local church. When one or more is emphasized to the exclusion or minimizing of others, you have problems," Paul said.

"What are the six areas?" Sharon asked him.

"Well, the Book of Acts shows that there were exciting qualities that later became a pattern for the Christians in the New Testament church.*

---

*Acts 2:42-47: "They met constantly to hear the apostles teach, and to share the common life, to break bread, and to pray. A sense of awe was everywhere, and many marvels and signs were brought about through the apostles. All whose faith had drawn them together held everything in common: they would sell their property and possessions and make a general distribution as the need of each required. With one mind they kept up their daily attendance at the temple, and, breaking bread in private houses, shared their meals with unaffected joy, as they praised God and enjoyed the favour of the whole people. And day by day the Lord added to their number those whom he was saving."

"First, they hungered for the Word of God. They studied Scripture and met to hear the apostles teach.

"Second, they met as a family for fellowship with other saints in the assembly.

"Third, as a group, they set aside a time for worship and praise for God.

"The fourth quality was their emphasis on prayer. Their conversations with God became important and were another means of uniting them.

"Giving, or stewardship, was the fifth characteristic of the early Christians. They shared so that anyone in their midst had his needs met.

"Finally," Paul said, "they witnessed to their world. And the Bible says they added new converts to their church—'day by day the Lord added to their number.'"

Sharon tried to absorb Paul's fervor at this new thought, listening as he explained.

"This is our example for balanced Christian lives and a balanced congregation. Through the years, either through doctrinal interests or denominational peculiarities, churches have emphasized one or more of these qualities to the exclusion of the others," Paul told his wife. "I think each 'whole' Christian and vital church will be the sum total of these six qualities."

"I think I see what you're saying," Sharon said. "In other words if we go overboard in any one area—whether it's fellowship or evangelism or whatever—we can get mixed up."

Paul nodded.

Sharon smiled. Her husband looked like anything but a preacher or philosopher as he sat under the shade of the beach umbrella. His sunglasses had slipped down over his nose and his forehead was peeling. His bright garish swim trunks almost made Sharon laugh as she thought of the incongruity of their setting and dialogue.

Before they flew back to New York, Paul—while in deep communion with God—felt that their retreat was a significant turning point in his career. Another concept came out of the retreat that was to shape his thinking.

One morning as Paul headed for his hammock by the beach, he picked up another book entitled *A Daily Guide to Miracles*. Written by Oral Roberts, the book fired Paul's heart and under the heading of "God's Prosperity Plan" in his journal, He began to write.

God has promises and provisions in His Word—a universal law of planting and harvest, sowing and reaping (Gal. 6:7).

God can bless you only to the degree that you have blessed others. It's His way to release His abundant blessings. And God *wants* to bless us and enjoys giving to us (Ps. 34:10, Eph. 3:20, Luke 6:38).

The Lord wants us to understand that *giving* is more for our benefit than His. Prosperity is *not* an accident. Miracles of supply do not happen by chance. There are important principles to learn.

1. *God Is Our Provider* (Phil. 4:19). As our Source, he supplies all needs. Most of our life we look to *horizontal* sources to supply our needs (parents, job, banks), but God wants us to learn we have a *vertical* Source who gives us all we need. God is bigger than the sum total of *all* our needs; He's so big He cannot fail (2 Cor. 9:8,9).

As our Provider, God wants us to glorify Him. He wants the world to know He is God through the miracles it sees Him doing in our lives (Prov. 11:24,25).

2. *Plant Seeds away from yourself in the soil of another's need.* A seed is *any resource* that you can willfully give away. By planting that "seed" in the "soil" of someone else's need, in *faith*, the eternal law ("whatsoever a man sows, that will he also reap") promises God's repayment.

3. *The Miracle of Harvest* (Luke 6:38). When we give, God gives in return. No wonder God says, ". . . Happiness lies more in giving than in receiving" (Acts 20:35). When you want or need a miracle, be a daresaint—"seed" your miracle. Give something of yours first. The seed will die, germinate, come alive in the "soil" of your planting, and become a plant full of fruit.

It is not selfish to give in order to get. *It is selfish only* if you're looking at horizontal sources instead of the true Source. When your giving, your "seeding," is done "as unto the Lord," your provisions will be *from* the Lord. And sparse sowing means sparse reaping (2 Cor. 9:6,7).

When Paul and Sharon returned from their retreat, things in the church were in good shape—spiritually. But the financial condition of the church was poor. A second TV telethon could not be held. The denomination had prevented them from using the mailing list from the previous telethon since it contained names of Nazarene donors from other churches. Paul was cautious about the future but not overly concerned. He came back with a measure of faith based on this new principle discovered during his and Sharon's retreat experience.

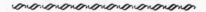

"There is a supernatural law of stewardship that the world can't understand," Paul preached back at the Lamb's. "That law is this: 'give . . . and it will be given to you,' pressed down and above all your expectations. There's also another side to this law: It is possible to hang on to something and end up with nothing. It is also possible to give, but in the act of giving, to actually *increase* what you have."

Paul went on to explain the principle of Luke 6:38 in practical terms. "If you give out of your own need, you will receive from God to supply your needs."

He paused and looked around. "I see Darren Cox sitting over there. He's the only other guy I know who is over six feet four inches and wears size forty-four extra long. Darren come up here, please. Now let me tell you what I have in mind. I guess it's no secret that your pastor is always broke. What little money we get goes right back into the ministry here at Lamb's. But I do have one good suit, and you're looking at it." There was a ripple of understanding laughter. Darren Cox had come up to the platform, not certain of what Paul was going to do.

"Darren, since you're on staff here at Lamb's I know that you're not one of the richest people in town, either," Paul remarked. Again there was an appreciative chuckle.

"Now, Darren, I'd like God to help me get a new suit. So I'm giving this suit to *you*. Here try on the jacket," Paul smiled.

"But, Pastor, I can't take your suit," Darren protested, as he slipped off his own jacket and tried on Paul's.

"Perfect fit," Paul observed. "Great. Darren, it's yours. I've only worn that suit a few weeks, and it's got a lot of wear left in it. I want you to have it."

Darren began to protest once more, but Paul waved down his objection. "I can't take 'no' for an answer, because with the principles God has demonstrated in Scripture about repaying, I'm expecting Him to give me at least two or three suits in return. So, if you don't take my suit, we both lose!"

Paul put his hand on Darren's shoulder and prayed, "Lord, honor me with Your Word. I'm 'planting' this suit in the soil of Darren's need, and I expect a miracle in my own life and need."

During the next few days several calls came. Edsel Stenstrom said, "Pastor, it'll look awfully funny if you don't get a suit now that you stuck your neck out! Meet me at Bond's and I'll buy you a suit."

While Paul was grateful for the new black pinstripe suit Edsel bought him, he knew this wasn't what God had in mind. He was right. Within a week Paul got phone calls from people *outside the church* who knew nothing about the Sunday sermon demonstration. They came from friends who "suddenly felt led" to buy Paul a suit or sport coat. By the end of the sermon series three weeks later, Paul had three suits and three sport coats from (except for Edsel) totally unexpected sources.

Paul put the concept to work in his family as well.

"Daddy, can we take a vacation to Disneyworld in Florida?" Sheri asked her father one day.

"Well, let's ask God. We don't have the money. We don't have a car, and it would cost a fortune to fly the whole family to Florida and back. Then we'll need motel rooms and meals. That's an enormous amount of money for us, but not for God. Shall we trust Him for it?" Paul asked.

The youngster eagerly said yes. But by July God had not come through with the money or tickets.

A call came to Paul from the director of one of the denomination's summer camps.

"Paul, we need someone to serve as counselor-pastor during a week of camp this month. It is next week, in fact. We're bringing in a group of underprivileged kids from the city and need extra help. Can you come?"

Paul thought of all the reasons why he could not help: He hated sleeping in canvas hammocks slung under flimsy cabin roofs. He didn't like hot days and cold nights. He hated bugs and camp food. There were other reasons, too. He had sermons to prepare, duties at his church, other responsibilities, and not enough time to rearrange his schedule.

But Paul thought of his seed faith principle. "I'll plant this as a seed toward a family vacation," he thought and agreed to serve the third week of July.

After he hung up the phone, Paul got down beside the sofa in his office to pray. "I'm sorry, Lord. That was a lousy attitude on my part. Those inner-city kids need this week. It doesn't matter if I have a few minor inconveniences when they have so many— all the time. Forgive my attitude and help me minister to them. I want to use this as an opportunity to plant my family's need for a vacation in the soil of those kids' needs. And I pray that . . ."

The telephone interrupted his prayer. He quickly finished and stood to answer it.

"Hello, Reverend Moore?" the caller asked.

"Yes."

"This is Bill Dooner in Tennessee," he continued. "We have a mutal friend, author Bill Proctor."

"Yes, Mr. Dooner, what can I do for you?"

"Bill said you'd be the one to help me out of a jam. I've been asked to guest-host a Knoxville TV show, and I need five guests for the last week of July. I'd like you to be one of them. Bill recommends you and your work most highly."

"Boy, ordinarily I'd be happy to. But we've been sort of planning our vacation for that week."

"Where are you going?" Dooner asked.

"We hope to visit Orlando and Disneyworld," Paul said.

Dooner asked, "Where will you be staying? Are you driving or flying?"

"I'm not sure. We don't have a car. We're trusting the Lord at this point," was Paul's weak reply.

The caller paused, then continued. "Well, that's interesting. You see, I own Scottish Inns of America and our number one franchise is in Orlando. Tell you what, if you'll come on my show, I'll fly you and your family to Knoxville. It'll only take a day out of your vacation. Then I'll get you a car for a couple of weeks. The TV show pays a modest fee, and I'll give you a letter that will put you up free at any Scottish Inn in the Southeast. You can charge your meals to the room. Now, you can't beat that, can you?"

Paul was flabbergasted. When he explained what had happened to his family, the children were wide-eyed at God's provision.

"I thought we'd have to go somewhere else and you'd say it wasn't God's will to go to Disneyworld if nothing happened with our prayer," Sheri admitted. "I believed God, but I didn't know if you and Mommy really believed God would get us to Disneyworld."

Paul fulfilled his promise at the camp, a week that saw rich spiritual results in the lives of inner-city kids. Paul knew he had made the right decision.

God fulfilled His part of the "repayment" when Paul and the family flew to Knoxville and Paul appeared on TV. After the show, Bill Dooner gave Paul an envelope with an introduction and due bill that gave them access to rooms and meals in Scottish Inns in Florida, Georgia, and the Carolinas. He also included keys to a rental car (also at no charge) and four one-hundred dollar bills for "incidentals."

Thirty-nine

JOE COLAIZZI WAS up before dawn and out walking the dew-covered fields by sunrise. Dolly's ragged terrier, Nip, playfully ran zig-zag patterns through the tall grass and chased back to Joe who was deep in prayerful thought.

He had taken time to "clear up loose ends," as he explained to Dolly. Now it was time to go.

Deeply moved by Moishe Rosen's New York challenge, Joe was convinced that God wanted him to be there—although he had no specific idea of *where* in New York.

His thoughts went back to his first days as a new Christian. He had such a small understanding of God's ways. All he knew was to *trust God,* that when he moved out in faith, God honored his motives and led him specifically.

"That's it," Joe said aloud. "I'll leave for New York with nothing, just as the early aspostles did and trust God to take me to where I'm supposed to be and to supply all my needs!"

The little brown dog stopped, cocked his head, and looked at Joe who laughed. "That doesn't make any sense to you, fella? Well, me neither. But God knows what's happening. I'm going to really step out in faith this time."

Dolly's family did not understand Joe's strange and mystical plan. But they knew better than to try to talk him out of it.

"Do you have money, and what about luggage?" Ron asked.

"It'll be easier to trust God completely than to try to cover everything," Joe told them. "The Scriptures tell of the apostles who went out as missionaries trusting in God. They were told to take 'no scrip (wallets or money), no clothes, no food.' I'm leaving in that same confidence," Joe announced.

Dolly's dad went into the den after breakfast and was gone

several minutes. He returned with a small sign fashioned from a manila file folder. Written with a broad felt-tip marker, it read: "New York."

"You can hold this up where you're 'thumbin,' " he told Joe. "And here, take this." He held out a five dollar bill. "I figure you mean business about havin' faith and all. But this is for emergencies. Take it for me, huh?"

Joe tried to protest, but Dolly's dad was insistent.

It wasn't long before Dolly drove up. Joe said his "good-byes" quickly and promised to stay in touch. Then he left with Dolly and rode toward the turnpike. Dolly said very little. When they were almost there, she said quietly, "I suppose we'll never see each other again, Joe C."

"Oh, I don't know. Maybe . . ."

"No, I don't think so. But I'm glad we both found Jesus before . . . before something bad, real bad happened to one of us. I want to thank you for witnessing to me and my family. We owe our salvation to your faithfulness," she said. It tumbled out so quickly and so orderly, he knew she must have rehearsed it on the way over. It was something she wanted him to know before he left.

They pulled off on the shoulder by the ramp leading to the Turnpike and said their good-byes. Dolly leaned over and kissed her former husband. It was not a lover's kiss, but a sister's farewell.

"God go with you, Joe C.," she said with eyes blinking back tears.

Ten minutes later, standing on the Turnpike waiting for a ride, Joe Colaizzi was aware of the five dollar bill in his pocket. He thought now of that money in his jeans. He took out the folded currency. It felt strange and represented, unconsciously, a lack of trust. He wasn't really trusting God.

Slowly he put the hand with the bill to his side. He opened his fingers and let it flutter away. He watched it blow across the concrete and land on a patch of grass missed by the mowers. Then the wind whipped again, and it blew down the slope of the access ramp and out of sight.

"Lord, that money is Yours. Give it to someone who needs it,"

Joe prayed. "And Lord, I pray for someone to stop who needs a word of witness," he added. As he opened his eyes, a Chevy station wagon slowed and stopped. The driver motioned for him to come and ride.

"Thank You, Jesus," Joe grinned and ran toward the car.

Paul's mother came to visit her son, Sharon, and the three grandchildren. Her visits were always happy cheerful events to which they all looked forward. Mrs. Moore had lived with Paul's youngest sister, Esther, after Paul's dad had died of cancer during the New Milford days.

His mother was quite proud of Paul's achievements and kept a scrapbook of clippings and his awards. She talked to everyone about his accomplishments. However, now in these later years, Paul's mom was more quiet and thoughtful. She suffered from an enlarged heart condition and had undergone a radical mastectomy following breast cancer. Her enlarged heart had caused the most difficulties for her, however, because it impaired her circulation. In the previous year, in fact, she had been hospitalized and had slipped into a coma, near death.

Miraculously, she had recovered. In the meantime she had lost nearly sixty-five pounds and had learned how to walk again.

Paul was deeply hurt by her pain and disease. Many times he felt guilty, as if he were somehow personally responsible. Not knowing the seriousness of her condition, he had asked "Grandma" to be babysitter for young "P.J." and accompany them on the cross-country tour with the multi-media spectacular. He was absolutely convinced, despite the doctors assurance to the contrary, that the strains of the trip had brought on his mother's illness.

Paul looked across the room at his mother playing with three-year-old Paul, Jr. Grandma was laughing and her eyes sparkled. But beneath the surface, Paul saw her tired spirits, her lack of strength. It pained him deeply to see his mother growing old and sick.

Paul's parents had always been a godly influence in his life. As a rebellious teenager, sneaking in after a night of "hell raising revelry," he had heard his parents on their knees praying for him—that the Lord would put His hand on their son, keep him, and make him a servant of God.

Paul knew that he had been brought up under the biblical guidelines of "train a child in the way he should go." He had learned the value of this Christ-centered tutoring in the things of God so consistently demonstrated by his parent's love and prayers. It was a heritage he promised to give his own children.

Paul also decided to tell his mom how much he loved and appreciated her.

The year 1976 is remembered for the American Bicentennial. To Paul and six young men from the church it brings back other memories.

Following the principles in the book *Master Plan for Evangelism,* which had affected Paul's thinking on his spring retreat, he had implemented a plan to spend twenty hours a week with six men who would give Paul a year of their lives. Paul had prayed that God would direct him to the right six men. Bob DiQuattro was one. He and another "seasoned" believer, along with four relatively new Christians had agreed to the experiment.

Paul worked on a schedule that gave him time with each of his "disciples." They shared his life. In much the same way he had learned from his father, they went along with Paul on his business. One at a time, each sat in as observers in counselling sessions, watched Paul prepare sermons, and listened as he talked on the phone.

Lessons in time management, doctrine, concepts of "The Exciting Church," or other principles were taught by Paul. He assigned important books—devotional, inspirational, theological—for them to read and report on, sharing with him and each other their insights and observations.

Paul delegated various church responsibilities to them. Each man recorded his thoughts and assignments and was required to report back to Paul. In so doing, the men developed a sense of accountability.

At the end of the year, each of the six men moved on into some area of active, full-time Christian service. Paul was greatly pleased with the experiment and felt the validity of the discipling concept had been proved.

Forty

A NOTHER PRINCIPLE DEVELOPED during Sharon and Paul's island vacation was put into practice during the summer and fall when Paul preached a series entitled—"Real Man, Real Woman, Real Marriage."

The essense of his teaching was that God created man, both men and women, in His own image (Gen. 1:27). Further, God had said, ". . . 'It is not good for the man to be alone. I will provide a partner for him' " (Gen. 2:18). ". . . the two become one flesh" (Gen. 2:24).

Paul told his congregation, "When God distributed His personality, character, godliness, and other qualities to men and women, He gave aspects of his being to men that He didn't give to women; he gave certain qualities to women that He didn't give to men. We see them now as masculine and feminine traits. This set up a natural bipolarity so that the human race could exist only in units of two—a one 'dual being' consisting of two distinct persons—one male, one female."

Paul went on to elaborate. "Each part of this dual being brings natural instincts, personality, emotions, and spiritual insights to the other. They complement each other. Men and women complement each other sexually. In every facet of work, play, and life, we see this natural law of completeness through complementary factors. And spiritually, the blending of masculine and feminine traits results in a maximum likeness of God; reproduction of His image in us can be realized best when man and woman are married and become one dual being, fulfilled through one another."

Paul's ideas on this topic brought initial tensions and questions from young career singles in the church who had considered themselves self-sufficient. They saw marriage as simply a choice, not an imperative for spiritual, physical, emotional, and intellectual fulfillment and completeness.

However, the series made its impact.

Steven, a gifted young artist, had come to Paul about this same time for counsel. He had been a homosexual and was trying to change his sexual orientation.

Paul explained how in God's natural order of bipolarity, only a heterosexual orientation was ordained by God.

"But I've never even dated a woman before," Steven confessed. "I don't like women. I'm uncomfortable with them."

Paul shook his head. "That's not true. I've see you talking with Joyce, the new dorm mother for the girls."

"Yeah, but she's more of a buddy," Steven said. "Besides . . . uh . . . she understands me."

"Because she was a lesbian before God saved her?" Paul asked bluntly.

"Maybe," Steven admitted quietly.

"Steven . . . listen to me. I believe God can reorient your sexual preferences. I want you to *date* Joyce. Dress up. Take her out to a fancy restaurant, pick up the tab, pull her chair out, help her with her coat, and open doors for her."

"But what's that going to do?" Steven asked.

"It's like planting a seed of faith. Joyce needs the attention and true affection of a man. You'll be ministering to her need, and God will repay you for it."

Although he'd always felt threatened by women, Steven was less frightened of Joyce. They agreed on a date. It was so successful and enjoyable that they planned another date. And another.

Their respect for each other as "buddies" turned to affection. Their closeness in each successful date demonstrated their separate traits and complementary characteristics.

Joyce and Steven, with their past homosexual attractions, were surprised—but pleased to see that a physical, sexual attraction for each other had now begun.

Joyce, whose inner hate and revulsion for all men still scarred her mind, had not kissed a man in nearly three years. Steven had never kissed a woman, except his mother.

Now, miraculously, they wanted to kiss each other. It was such a special moment, they paused to pray. They thanked God for His gift of grace that had changed and redeemed their backgrounds and brought them to this moment where they felt natural sexual attractions.

In so many ways their first kiss was very special.

Before long, Joyce and Steven announced their engagement.

❧❧❧❧❧❧❧❧❧❧❧❧❧

The "Real Man, Real Woman" principles had taken root in the lives of many couples in the church. Before long, Paul found himself performing a wedding nearly every weekend.

John Hillyer and Beverly Irving were married in a beautiful candlelight ceremony. Jim and "Dusty" Hullinger were also wed, as were Wayne and Jo Ellen Rogers, Joseph Bruccoleri and Barbara Billings.

Peter Pasqualino, having experienced the agony of divorce along with the futility of a hopeless reconciliation, met, fell in love with, and married Elise, a lovely Christian nurse. A total of thirty couples were married following Paul's series. But perhaps the greatest proof of the principle of the "Real Man, Real Woman" relationship—and a miracle in its own right—was the wedding held in the parsonage at 231 East Thirty-second Street.

With Paul in front of them, the man and woman stood quietly, savoring the assurance of God's abundant love for them. The days of cult-induced guilt, a desperate kidnapping, a two-continent separation, a badly broken communication, seemed far distant. Now all was mended and restored. More than one prayer of thanksgiving and praise slipped silently from the lips of those watching as Bob and Esther DiQuattro looked at one another in love and vowed to be husband and wife.

Forty-one

PAUL QUIETLY TOOK his place at the monthly board meeting. He knew in advance what the main topic of discussion would be. The financial crisis was building. Bills amounting to more than $70,000 needed to be paid. There was no money for payroll, nor had there been since early summer. It was now late August, and the staff had not been paid for nearly three months. They had pooled whatever income they had, including savings, just to keep going. Church members donated food and financial support.

Somehow they would keep going until a miracle happened. But twelve weeks had gone by *without* a miracle.

Paul read over the gloomy report. They were three months behind in all their bills and had no hope of seeing their way through September, let alone the rest of the year. He sat there for several moments, listening as the group's discussion went from concern to despair. Finally, he spoke.

"Okay. I want to make a motion that we sell the Lamb's." The unspeakable had been spoken. "I think this is the only course of action available to us in light of the circumstances," Paul continued. "I know some of you are hesitant to make such a suggestion because you know what this place means to all of us. Is there a second?"

No one spoke.

Paul went on, "Look, as an ultimate act of trust, we'll sell the building on September 7 if God doesn't supply our needs by

September 6. We need $70,000 in cash for past due payables and at least $50,000 in pledges to get us through the next couple of months."

"All right, I'll second the motion to sell," one of the men said.

In the discussion that followed Paul proposed some plans. "We'll have one more attempt at fund raising. September 3, 1976, is our third anniversary. That's Labor Day. We'll plan a big 'D-Day' fund raising event to raise the money. We'll tell the people in our letter that we're trusting God to tell us through them whether He wants us to sell the Lamb's. We'll open the letters on 'D-Day,' and if there's not $70,000 in cash and $50,000 in pledges, we'll return the checks. There's enough equity in the Lamb's to bail us out. It'll be our fleece, God's way of telling us what we should do."

It was nine days before the big fund raising event. Mark Weimer supervised the final mail drop. Not even enough money had been available to run off a computer list, so the thousands of letters had to be hand addressed.

As their leader, Paul had tried to maintain an optimistic outlook. Although they were not beaten, it was getting harder to combat the gloom. Even he was getting more discouraged. It really seemed hopeless. With the excitement of a telethon beamed at over 1.5 million homes, they had raised $300,000. Now with nothing but a letter to a small donor list, they were expecting to raise $125,000. It looked impossible.

All the Scripture promises and encouragements Paul had used in the past to keep his people trusting God for miracles seemed to be hollow, mocking. Paul's faith was haggard.

He got up and went over to the window in his office and looked out.

"Oh, God," Paul prayed, "don't give up on us now."

Look outside . . . across the street, an inner voice suggested.

Across the street was the Hudson Theater, scene of one of their most dramatic victories. Formerly a pornographic movie house, because of Paul and the Lamb's, it was now showing G-rated family films.

Wasn't that "impossible" a year ago?

"But, Lord, I'm beaten, discouraged," Paul prayed.

Leave your office and take a walk.

Paul went downstairs and walked a half block to the cacophony of Times Square. He strode quickly across the street, dodging pedestrians and traffic, to Duffy Square on the north where Forty-fourth Street crosses—past the U.S. Armed Forces recruiting booth.

For a moment he stood and looked all around him, above him, beside him. Many layers of emotion were touched—excitement, concern, loneliness, despair, hope in Christ.

Wasn't this hope the reason you came to Manhattan?

Paul stood beside a big concrete planter. In an attempt to beautify Times Square, the city fathers had placed eight of these planters, each with a lovely tree inside, on the sidewalks. Usually they were unnoticed. Often they became litter receptacles. The trees themselves never adjusted to this hostile environment of dirt, darkness, decay, exhaust fumes, and pollution. They died and had to be replaced every six months or so.

"Maybe that's what happens to churches and Christians in New York, too," Paul mused. He looked up and down the busy boulevards. He saw no shortage of funds here. The nodding junkie across the street somehow got his hands on $150 a day to support his drug habit. The businessman who spent $50 on lunch and drinks had no worries about money. The man who visited the massage parlor on Forty-fourth Street had no misgivings about spending $40 or $50 for a few minutes of casual sex. Even the sex shops and bookstores seemed to have a profitable turnover of customers.

"But where do we go to get help for Your work, Lord?" Paul agonized.

Look around you; what do you see?

Paul looked at the flashing Coke sign, the huge Seagram's marquee, the famous Camel cigarette sign with the smoke rings. He saw the people and the crying needs of the city and knew his calling.

This is your parish.

"I know You called me here, Lord. But God," Paul prayed, "how are You going to *keep* us here?"

Almost as if in answer, Paul heard the chirp of a small bird. He looked down and saw a sparrow. A napkin was laid out like a miniature picnic tablecloth in the dirt of one of the concrete tree containers. The napkin was spread with bread crumbs, and the sparrow was eating contentedly and chirping a song of gratefulness.

Paul saw an old "bag lady" wandering slowly between the potted trees and spreading napkins and bread crumbs on each one.

What is a sparrow worth? Yet, you see God cares for even the least of His creatures. Are not His children of more value than sparrows? Don't worry about the future. It's in God's hands.

∽∽∽∽∽∽∽∽∽∽∽∽∽∽

A thousand envelopes had arrived in the mail before "D-Day," September 3. Paul waited to open them.

"We are indeed trusting God. He has demonstrated in so many ways that He cares for us," he explained to a reporter. "That's why I'm not afraid to invite the press to our 'D-Day' event. We'll set up a table for reporters and a place for TV cameras. The church officers will be in the front of the church counting the checks, using adding machines and calculators to keep track of the amounts. We'll return all the money if we don't make our goal. But we don't believe God wants us to sell the Lamb's," Paul said.

D-Day was to be an all-day rally. The church was packed by two o-clock when the congregation met to learn the decision regarding their future as a church.

Chuck Blake, George Gressett, Ken Huber, and Jim Hullinger supervised as eight calculators were set up on tables at the front of the church.

There were five telephone lines for incoming calls. Everyone was expectant, anxious.

In an expression of faith, Judi Cochran sang a solo, "Thank You, Lord for What You've Done." Rita McLaughlin, an actress from the network TV series, *As The World Turns,* also sang.

Reverend Scutt was present to lend his support to their efforts.

Paul led the service, which began with the announcement of a $15,000 grant from CBN's Pat Robertson. The sparse mail brought more checks, but they were still substantially short of the goal. The reason, they decided, was because the Labor Day weekend mail was still in the post office.

Paul asked Mark Weimer to somehow get their mail released. Mark called the New York postmaster at his suburban home and, in spite of rules and regulations, convinced him to call their local post office to release the mail. Mark jubilantly returned with several sacks, praising the Lord as he entered the church. These added to the cash and pledges, but they were still short.

The five phones were kept busy taking pledges. Close to the end of the rally, they announced a pledge from Bill Bright's Campus Crusade for Christ for $15,000 and a $6,000 gift from Vic Diffy in Oklahoma, marked "special delivery."

Yet, they were still $10,200 short. Then, just before nine o'clock, a check for $10,000 arrived, followed by smaller amounts putting them over the goal.

When all the envelopes were opened, the checks and pledges tallied, the treasurer stood to read his report. "We have $87,000 in cash and $57,000 in pledges—a total of $144,000!"

It was enough to pay their bills, take care of back salary for the staff, and get them back on their feet financially. Everyone was overjoyed.

One of the board members reasoned that now would be a good time to talk with Paul about the continuing financial matters of the church. "There are two things I see in this situation," he told Paul. "One, no one can argue any more about whether God is in this work or not. He *is*. But secondly, I believe He expects us to be good stewards and businessmen as well. We need to put our house in order."

"What do you suggest?" Paul asked his friend.

"First, we have to define who we are. We think of ourselves as an urban missions project. That's the way the work began. The denomination has some leaders who think of us as another district church—yet we have no local board. We're governed by the district as a home missions work. In essence, we have a stalemate. The brethren in Kansas City say 'Raise your own support—become self-sufficient.' But when we try, we're crowding in on other Nazarene churches for support money."

"It sounds hopeless," Paul mused. "We've been going back and forth on this for years now."

Anyhow, the next step is to get a strong fund-raising and financial base," Paul's friend said.

"What's your idea?" Paul asked.

"Let's make the Lamb's a real 'urban missions center'—different from a local church or a district, yet denominational in character and structure. Let's keep it a place where our seminary students can be trained. Let's end the hasssle once and for all. We'll establish an 'Office of Urban Mission Affairs,' and ask Kansas City to bring in a professional administrator to run it. Then, you can be the local minister, appointed to the New York congregation."

Paul liked the concept and along with Reverend Scutt, George Gressett, Chuck Blake, and Ron Mercer worked on an official proposal to take to Kansas City in December.

Forty-two

FOR SEVERAL WEEKS Joe Colaizzi had walked the streets of New York, waiting for God to indicate why He had called him to this city.

Meanwhile, just as he had witnessed of his faith to a salesman, a truck driver, and an elderly couple while hitchhiking from Pennsylvania, Joe continued to share his faith.

A black derelict stopped him on the corner and asked for a handout.

"Man, I don't have any money. But I've got something better." Joe told him about the change Jesus had made in his life.

The black man listened and asked questions of Joe about his experiences. As they walked along the street they were approached by a younger black man who recognized the derelict. He seemed to be drunk and had been crying.

"What's the matter, Herby? You in trouble?" his older friend asked.

"Yeah, Sonny. I'm in *bad* trouble," Herby cried. "I just had a fight in the bar with my ol' lady. I was drunk and we started arguin.' I took out my knife to scare her, y'know. An' first thing I know, I cut her."

"How bad?" Sonny asked.

"Real bad. Maybe eight or ten times I stabbed her."

"Jeez," the old man whispered. "What you gonna do?"

"I'm thinking about jumpin' in front of a train before I sober up and change my mind!" Herby told them. Then, noticing Joe, he asked, "Do I know you?"

Joe shook his head and smiled, offering his hand. "I'm Joe Colaizzi. Sonny and I were talking about Jesus when we ran into you. Sounds to me like you need Jesus," Joe said plainly. "Jumping in front of a train won't help."

Herby began to cry again. "I didn't mean to cut her. I'm sorry, baby. I'm sorry . . ."

"Did someone call for help?" Joe asked the man.

He nodded. "Police was called first, and I ran away. But I waited down the block, scared. Then an ambulance come and took her."

"Was your wife conscious when they took her away?"

"Yeah. She was screamin' and cussin' and callin' for me. She was alive, all right. But . . ." Herby broke down again.

This time Sonny spoke. "Say, how's about we go home to my place. We can talk there. You guys can stay the night at my place. It's warmer there than here on the street. What d'ya say?"

Joe and Herby nodded, and they started to walk to the bus stop. Joe said, "Tomorrow, you'll be sober and we can talk about this. We'll help you do the right thing, Herby. I think Jesus will give you an answer. I'm going to pray for you and your wife, Herby."

"Uh . . . anyone got money for the bus?" Joe asked, knowing he had absolutely nothing himself. The others shook their heads also.

"Then we can't take the bus," Joe said.

"Sure we can," said Sonny, flagging down the approaching bus. It stopped and Sonny pushed the other two on before following them. The black driver looked at the trio and determined they had no money.

"We have had hard times, brother," Sonny explained.

The driver nodded and waved them on.

∽∽∽∽∽∽∽∽∽∽∽∽∽

Hardly a day passed without someone coming to Christ through Joe Colaizzi's simple witness. He covered an area of Forty-second Street where he spoke to pimps, prostitutes, drifters, and dope pushers. Some resented his intrusion into their existence. But others welcomed his friendly, effective concern. Sometimes he went over to the Port Authority Bus Terminal and talked with military men on leave, cruising homosexuals, runaways, and other street people. They usually listened and responded to his presentation of Jesus Christ. "After all," he argued, "if he can change a person like me, he can help anyone."

For someone on the street, that was his most effective argument. Many of them had heard some kind of preaching before. Most ministers, they felt, were too far removed from their scene to really identify and relate to them. Joe was one of their own, one who had touched bottom and climbed back up, who had earned the right to be heard and trusted.

The street people around Forty-second Street nicknamed him "Preach." He survived on God's strength and some napping at the Port Authority. But it was getting too cold to live on the streets. Joe fought off discouragement and impatience, wondering why God was still silent as to his mission. Was he to be indefinitely an itinerant street preacher with no place of his own? Then one day the answer came—from unexpected quarters.

"Hey, Preach! How you doin' today?"

"I'm doing okay, by God's grace. How are you Bobby?"

"I'm okay, too," Bobby replied. Bobby, a bouncer at a Forty-second Street bar, was friendly toward Joe. "Hey, Preach, I've been wonderin'—are you with those Jesus freaks over on Forty-fourth?"

"Jesus freaks?" Colaizzi asked.

"The ones who took over the old Lamb's Club. Don't you know about 'em? You ought to go look 'em up."

Paul finished his Bible study and dismissed the Wednesday night prayer meeting with a brief prayer and benediction. Several clusters of people, in groups of two and three, stayed to chat as others went their way.

Paul was looking for Sharon so they could leave. His mother was in the hospital again, and he wanted to call when they got home to check on her condition. Tomorrow he'd go and visit her.

SHEPHERD OF TIMES SQUARE

On his way toward the back of the room, Paul noticed a quiet stranger. He'd seen him during the service several times. The man was not unaccustomed to church services. He carried a Bible and seemed to enter into the praying and singing as well.

Upon closer inspection, Paul saw that the man was tired and needed a rest. His eyes were bloodshot and swollen, probably from lack of sleep. He went up to the man and stuck out his hand. "Hello, brother. My name's Paul Moore . . . what's your story?"

The man looked up. Though his features were haggard, his face was friendly, his smile warm. "Reverend Moore . . . my name's Joe Colaizzi . . . and God brought me here by way of Pittsburgh and Santa Fe. It's quite a story."

"Well, Joe," Paul smiled. "Why don't you let me get a couple fellas from the Lamb's here to show you where you can clean up and get a meal. We've got some room—a place to stay for a few days until you get on your feet. We'll give you a bed, hot shower, shave, some clean clothes, and dinner. Then, why don't you get a good night's sleep and tell me your story tomorrow?"

"Sounds good to me, Reverend Moore!" Joe said with a smile.

ᘛᘖᘛᘖᘛᘖᘛᘖᘛᘖᘛᘖᘛᘖᘖ

As shepherd of his flock, Paul was somewhat accustomed to hospitals, having visited members of his congregation when they were injured or sick.

But it was something else this time, less clinical. His mother was here, steadily growing weaker. She had been making good progress since last year when she had been hospitalized and in a coma. She was walking much better now, without the aid of a walker. His mother had even come to the "D-Day" event in September and stayed for most of the counting. She had sat in the auditorium with a white shawl draped over her shoulders, gently encouraging her son through prayer.

Paul wished now that he had asked someone to take her home on "D-Day." Again he began to blame himself for what had happened. His mind went back to the bus tour, and the guilt he was holding against himself. But he knew he couldn't have stopped her from coming.

He went into his mother's room and stood beside her bed. She was sleeping lightly, unaware of his presence. Paul looked around the room. There were the usual cards and flowers, and a few small Christmas decorations. The holidays were only two weeks away.

His mind went back to another time, ten years earlier, when he had been in a hospital, praying that his infant daughter Cathi would not die from a rare blood disease.

Paul was comforted as he remembered the miracle that had saved her life. Now Cathi was a growing, healthy young girl. Perhaps God would intervene again for his mother.

Paul picked up her hand and pressed it into his own big hand. Tears welled up in his eyes; there were so many things to ask her. But he knew it was too late. The doctors could do no more. She was in God's care now.

Paul sat down in a wooden chair beside the hospital bed, aware that his mother was dying.

ღღღღღღღღღღღღ

It was several weeks before Paul had the long chat with Joe Colaizzi and heard his full story. Entranced, he listened to the account of God at work. Joe told of Dolly, her family, of the black men Sonny and Herby, and of dozens of other "street people" whom he had brought to Christ. And Joe's "miracle-a-day" life had continued at the Lamb's. They had given Joe space in the basement to stay temporarily. The day after his arrival he had made himself busy using his carpentry skills, fixing, and cleaning.

Immediately, the staff had seen Joe's potential, not only in his handiwork, but in his "heart" work. When people came into the Lamb's from the street in trouble or in need, they seemed to gravitate to Joe—and he to them. There was an unspoken spirit between them. He understood their hurts first-hand and, more than a college-trained intern or church-taught staff leader, Colaizzi's gaze cut through the layers of bravado or "jive" to the core of the person's problem. The staff had seen his ability with people in need and had told Paul.

Paul, too, could see Joe's intellect and love for people as assets God could use at the Lamb's.

"Joe, we want you to stay and help us here," Paul said.

"I know," Joe replied. "God already spoke to me about it. I knew when I got here that this is why I came to New York. I just waited for Him to tell you!"

At Christmas, Joe Colaizzi wrote a long letter to his own family. It took him a long time to explain how God had brought him from the insanity of drugs to peace in Christ, and service for Him at the Lamb's.

"I'm involved in what they call a 'benevolence ministry,' " Joe wrote. "I work with one of the staff members of the church, and we minister mostly to the needs of street people. I've been here since . . ." He paused to check the calendar to see when he had arrived at the Lamb's so he could include the information in his letter home. Joe's eyes widened and he was suddenly overcome. He wept when he learned that the day God had brought him to the Lamb's was his *birthday*. Alone in the city, no one had known it was his special day. And in his confusion, even he had forgotten. But God had not overlooked his birthday.

Forty-three

IN DECEMBER, RON Mercer flew to Kansas City with Reverend Scutt to present the proposal to create two separate entities: first, a Nazarene church in Manhattan; and, second, an "Urban Missions Center" at the Lamb's. The denomination's leaders voted favorably on the recommendation and put the matter on the agenda for the annual general board meeting in January.

A month later, Ron called Paul with the exciting news. "The General Board voted unanimously to buy the Lamb's! It'll be their building; they'll run it, and we'll help with the various ministries. It's the perfect solution," Ron extolled.

"And the answer to three years of prayer," Paul reminded him. Paul mailed a copy of the proposal to creditors telling them, "Look at this; we'll be able to pay our bills in full in thirty days!"

In February, Raymond Hurn, the Executive Secretary of the Department of Home Missions, spoke to the congregation at Manhattan Church and explained the proposal.

"This is a new day of unprecedented cooperation to accomplish a common task," he said. "We are buying the building from you, but it is *your* building. We are providing administrative leadership and staff, but they are *your* staff. This is an exciting new day for the Lamb's!" The congregation jumped to their feet, weeping, shouting, and cheering. It was an explosive, emotional release. Debts would be paid in full. A staff of qualified professionals were coming to help. Competent students would serve as interns. At last there would be financial stability. It was too good to be true!

In March, a ten-member group came from Kansas City to do a

feasibility study, called for in the proposal passed by the General Board in January. The board had asked for a group to make recommendations on the "uses and control of operations" of the Lamb's.

Meanwhile, the monthly expenses were mounting again. Paul called on Kansas City to hurry the transfer and make funds available.

By April, all the paperwork was brought up to date so a closing could be made. Ron Mercer, the men of the board, and Reverend Scutt had met, drawn up all the necessary documents, prepared for transfer of deed and payoff figures, and then flown to Kansas City to finalize the transfer.

A call came from Kansas City. It was Reverend Scutt.

"Paul, meet us at the airport! Get ready for some pretty bad news." He hung up before Paul could question him.

On the drive to LaGuardia, Paul wondered what could be so bad. He met the men at the gate.

"The people at Kansas City have backed off! They're not going ahead with the transfer," they told a bewildered Paul.

Paul stared in disbelief, speechless.

Reverend Scutt explained what had taken place. The general superintendents of the General Church Board had heard the Lamb's proposal by Reverend Scutt and had been in favor of it. The plan would be a commitment to urban missions.

The plan had been approved by the General Board, subject to a feasibility study to recommend uses and control.

Gordon Olson, respected chairman of the finance committee of the General Board, had addressed the board in getting the proposal approved. Olson, a distinquished layman, held the confidence and respect of the entire denomination. What he had to say carried a great deal of weight in the decision. He had told the board, "I've been at the Lamb's and visited the Manhattan Church. I've sensed an unusual Christian spirit there. They are doing a great work and we must relieve them of their financial stress. I recommend we vote to buy the Lamb's!"

It was his speech in January that had caused the General Board to vote to do just that.

But two weeks later, Gordon Olson had died of a heart attack; and with him had ended the financial leadership and guidance of implementing that vote, because the board had voted approval with the idea that the funds were in the general budget.

It was an incredible oversight that no one had checked out, but the funds had *not* been in the budget. And no one, except perhaps Gordon Olson, knew where to get them. The lack of funds, along with a negative report from the feasibility study committee, had killed their hopes. The Nazarenes could not help Paul after all.

ᗡᖇᓂᗡ᠊ᖇᓂ᠊ᗡ᠊ᖇᓂ᠊ᗡ᠊ᖇᓂ᠊ᗡ᠊ᖇᓂ᠊ᗡ᠊ᖇᓂ᠊ᗡ

Paul was numb for a week following this terrible news. He understood the problems of the men in Kansas City but felt "they" had not kept their word. His staff and church were stunned, hurt, and angry.

"But, Pastor, we were told that headquarters was going to buy the Lamb's. What's going on?"

During the weeks and months that followed, there was a "blackout" of communications between the denomination and Paul Moore. No one called him; nor did he feel like calling anyone "over there." Even Reverend Scutt hesitated to call and discuss the matter. Paul didn't know exactly what had happened, but he felt betrayed, and didn't know what to do.

There began to be an undercurrent of "we/they" in discussions. Church people asked if the Manhattan Church was really all that committed to staying Nazarene in organization.

The only word that filtered down to Paul from the denomination was "Sell the Lamb's and dismiss your staff. We'll pay for your salary and a secretary, but anyone else either has to be self-supporting or a volunteer."

"Let's accept the fact that our denomination already gave us $140,000 and can't give us any more just now," Paul told his flock. "But I remember my dad always telling me, 'where God guides, God provides.' Let's find ways to cut back and find new ways to fund our work. Let's stay away from the sources we've tried before; we're losing our credibility with them, always begging for money, always talking about a crisis. We have to work toward new financial stability and integrity."

"I know of no other reason why Satan is trying to destroy us except that we are destined for a great future ministry in the power of God's Spirit. And I, for one, won't quit!" Paul exclaimed.

He told them about the last time he chose to give up in a situation exactly like this.

"When we were back in New Jersey, I had a vision for a work like this in Hackensack. I found a perfect place to locate the ministry," he explained. "It was the old Elks Club. The building was perfect with a ballroom, kitchen, grill room, residence and dormitory rooms, a sanctuary, and even a bowling alley. It was absolutely ideal for what we wanted. We developed a practical plan to acquire the building and start a ministry there.

"Then we ran into some obstacles with the city and zoning difficulties. We lost the building. I can still remember the sick feeling in my gut as I watched the big wrecking ball demolish that building. It was my own personal 'holocaust' in the sense that I promised myself 'never again!' I believe we should have held on, worked harder, and fought Satan for that building. It was contrary to God's purposes to see that wrecking ball smash a dream of the Holy Spirit."

Paul looked into the faces of his listeners. "Never again, brothers and sisters; never again. I refuse to give up."

Forty-four

PAUL WAS NOW forced to give fund raising a higher priority. He alone felt responsible for raising the money needed to operate the Lamb's. He made the rounds of all the foundations that he thought might take an interest in their work. Most of them, however, gave only limited grants, and generally to long-established works. "It takes a year to convince these foundation administrators that you're for real," Paul complained to Sharon one evening after an unsuccessful day.

"Where are you going tomorrow?" she asked.

"I'm going to see Walter Hoving of Tiffany's," Paul replied.

"But I've heard that he only gives to the Walter Hoving Home for Girls, where we send some of the prostitutes who come in looking for help," Sharon said.

"Yes, that's true. But I have an idea I want to discuss with him. You know the idea he had for the pin 'Try God'? He had a bunch of them made up by Tiffany's and sells them. All the proceeds go to the girl's home. Well, I want to talk to him about creating a pin with a different slogan to *sell* to some organization—you know, a Tiffany pin that says 'Jesus is Lord' or 'God loves you,' something like that."

"How would that help?" Sharon asked.

"I'd sell the pins to different companies or organizations and get a sales commission from Tiffany's. Actually, I'd just be an agent for the Lamb's, but one or two big sales could help us," Paul said.

The next day Paul met with the eighty-year-old president of Tiffany's in his elegant New York office. What Sharon had said was true—all of his giving was exclusively channelled to his Girls'

Home. But Hoving listened to Paul's proposal and agreed to let him become a special representative of Tiffay's to sell custommade pins to companies and organizations for a twenty-five-cent commission on each unit sold.

During their more general discussion, Paul realized that it might be wise for the Lamb's to form a nonprofit foundation both for tax purposes and to increase the efficiency and accountability of fund-raising efforts for the ministry.

Paul's mind raced with ideas as he said goodbye to Mr. Hoving and rode the elevator to the street.

〜〜〜〜〜〜〜〜〜〜〜〜〜

Jim Hullinger and Paul met several days later to discuss the possibility of creating a foundation to encompass the various ministries of the Lamb's.

"What do you plan to do?" Jim asked.

"I'm proposing that we form a 'Lamb's Ministries, Inc.' as a nonprofit foundation whose purpose will be to disperse grants for urban missions."

"I see," Jim observed.

"We'll call it LMI and it'll incorporate several of our existing areas of ministry: *crisis care, residential programs, theater programs, Sanctuary Restaurant and concert ministry,* and whatever else God calls into being.

The various LMI ministries were defined and spelled out:

Crisis Care was an extension of the 'benevolence' ministry of the Manhattan Church. Joe Colaizzi's intelligence, combined with "street savvy," made him an effective director of this area of outreach. In a desire to avoid duplicating an existing ministry, the Crisis Care Center cooperated with Teen Challenge (drugs), the Salvation Army, (poor people), Walter Hoving Home for Girls, (runaways, teen prostitutes), as well as city agencies and other Christian organizations. The Lamb's Crisis Care Center maintained a counselling center, a twenty-four-hour "help" hotline, a food kitchen for the hungry, and a clothing store for people in need.

The *Residential Program* was a place to provide housing and a sense of community for interns. It gave seminary students the practical benefits of living and working together in the Lamb's. However, the program also provided help for new Christians needing to get on their feet; help for emotionally disturbed people in need of a substitute for a broken, fragmented family; or help and rehabilitation for a young man or woman who would be swallowed up by "the street" if forced to go back too soon.

The Sanctuary Restaurant was an extension of the old Inner Light Gospel Cafe in which singles and couples of the church could invite their nonchurched friends to an evening of entertainment (concerts) and dinner with a gospel emphasis.

Paul also had dreams for organizing the young artists, actors, and actresses of the church and Christian community into a New York Christian Theater Company. There had been the beginning of such a project whenever these people got together to perform in church or prepare something for performance elsewhere—such as the multi-media spectacular, A New Way of Living, and the I Care TV Special.

So far as organization and creative development were concerned, Paul knew where he was going. Getting there was always the struggle.

Paul was now eager to sell some the Tiffany pins. He knew that the Oral Roberts Evangelistic Association in Tulsa, Oklahoma, was a large and well-respected Christian organization and decided to make them his first sales contact. Paul made up a sterling silver pin with the words "Expect a Miracle," feeling confident that the organization would order them for their constituency.

When he arrived on the campus of Oral Roberts University, Paul went to the corporate headquarters. He was greeted warmly by the people in the organization, and they listened attentively to his presentation.

However, they explained to Paul that they could not use the

pin idea. They preferred using Oral Roberts's books as give-aways to their donors and friends, since these had a proven effectiveness and ministry.

"But we'll call you if we ever change our minds," Paul's host said graciously as they stood to shake hands when the interview ended.

A little discouraged, Paul walked across the campus to the famous ORU Prayer Tower and went up to the top to look out. From there Paul could see all the buildings that had recently come into being—new science and medical buildings for the training of Christian doctors and nurses, dormitories, class-rooms, and a number of other educational facilities.

It was somehow encouraging to see how God had blessed one man's dream. *Oral Roberts is the 'patron saint' of seed faith*, Paul reminded himself, *and I've forgotten the basic principle of seed faith . . . that God is my Source.*

Paul's spirits brightened. He conversed many moments with God, while looking out across the campus. God seemed to speak to him: *If I can do all this for Oral Roberts, I can meet your needs too. You may have come here to sell a pin to temporarily ease your financial struggles, but stop looking for horizontal sources. Look to Me—you need a vertical Source. 'I shall supply all that you are wanting for according to My riches through Jesus Christ.'* Remember, I am your Source.*

Paul's heart was both excited and joyful. He felt very emo-tional at this moment and lingered in prayer for some time before leaving the tower.

ᕕᕗᕕᕗᕕᕗᕕᕗᕕᕗᕕᕗᕕᕗᕕᕗ

After his first presentation, Paul met with Joel Tucciarone. As an account executive for the Madison Avenue advertising firm of Wunderman, Ricotta & Kline, Inc., Joel had an idea that a Tiffany pin might be a good premium for Spiegel, Inc., a fa-mous mail-order catalogue house and one of his company's clients.

Joel arranged for a presentation to Henry Johnson, chairman

*Philippians 4:19.

of the board of Spiegel, Inc., at Hoving's office at Tiffany & Co. Walter Hoving and Paul were there to discuss the plan.

"Hank" Johnson listened attentively and, when Paul finished, said, "I like the concept. But I'm not convinced it should have a religious message like the one Mr. Hoving proposes—'God Loves You.'"

Paul answered, citing the benefits of the tie-in with Tiffany & Co. which would lend prestige to the campaign. "Also," he added, "it's for your Christmas catalogue cover. We think a religious emphasis at Christmas is appropriate."

"Besides," Walter Hoving interrupted, "it *has* to be a religious or patriotic message if it's going to be successful."

Paul squirmed and wished Hoving had not been quite so blunt.

"Well, how about 'rejoice'?" Johnson asked. That's not exactly the same as your slogan, but look how well it would look in the art treatment. Besides it wouldn't be offensive.

Paul thought about the idea. The layout called for a miniature Christmas tree, decorated only with the Tiffany & Co. pin. It was to go out on three million catalogue covers. The pin was to be a premium for buyers who bought a certain amount of merchandise.

"Yeah, I can see 'rejoice' on there. It's got a Christmas sound—a religious touch," he observed.

Again Hoving spoke up. " 'Rejoice' is awful. Anyone can say 'rejoice'—a drunk in a bar can yell 'rejoice.' You need to say 'God Loves You.' Don't be afraid of it!" Then he told Johnson the story of how the staid and prestigious Tiffany & Co. used his own 'Try God' pin. "You couldn't *buy* the prestige and good will we've gotten from that pin. There have been hundreds of thousands sold. It's helped me fund the Walter Hoving Home for Girls. And you know why? Because God *blessed* that pin. Now you use 'God Loves You' on your catalogue cover, and God will bless *your* business. I know it."

Oh, boy, we've blown it, thought Paul.

Johnson was silent for a moment, and then said, "All right. I guess I can go with 'God Loves You.' I trust Mr. Hoving's judgment on this. But I'll have to send it through our men in advertising. Ted Spiegel, our vice-president of marketing, needs to be involved in this decision, too."

Hank Johnson stood to leave. He extended his hand, first to Mr. Hoving, and then to Paul. "We'll put this past our people as quickly as we can. We should have a decision in a month or so at the latest."

Forty-five

PAUL HAD CUT staff and overhead as much as possible in order to meet the bills. He was working constantly on fund raising, with minimal success. Without denominational help or the ability to go to the television constituency for funds, they could not catch up.

Paul's biggest problem was with the electric utility conglomerate, Consolidated Edison. Con Ed had been overcharging the Lamb's ever since the church had bought the six-story building. The Lamb's should have been exempt from certain taxes, but Con Ed had been collecting them anyway. This, plus a combination of faulty meters in the steam room, had escalated the utility bills beyond reason.

Paul protested and went to court to remedy the situation. Meanwhile, the church would withhold monthly payments to Con Ed until the situation was corrected. The Public Service Commission intervened on behalf of Lamb's Ministries. The charge for taxes was dropped, and the faulty meters were replaced, the Lamb's Ministries was credited for the overcharge. Nevertheless, the church still owed Con Ed $45,000 even after the settlement.

The utility company demanded immediate payment of at

least half the amount and a plan to pay off the balance and remain current, or they threatened to turn off the service.

While Paul hopelessly struggled to raise the money, Con Ed obtained legal approval from the Public Service Commission to shut off electrical service to the Lamb's. They sent representatives to post notices in the lobby and mailed registered letters to the residents of the building, warning that within ten days electrical service to the building would stop.

In spite of the ongoing crisis, Paul still had responsibilities as pastor of the Manhattan Church. He tried to use the occasion to teach the spiritual principles he had always taught by finding God's truth in contemporary problems.

He was invited to preach in Brooklyn at Rev. Roy Brown's church. They had become good friends when Paul served as chairman for the "Here's Life, New York" evangelistic campaign, for which Reverend Brown had been a committee member.

Paul decided to preach on the seed faith concept at the all-black church. Reverend Brown's church had recently purchased new pews for their church, but Paul had learned that they needed more money to make the next payment on them or would risk losing them.

"Using the seed faith principle of planting in the soil of someone else's need," Paul told Reverend Brown's congregation, "our own church wants to demonstrate our faith in God. We have extreme financial problems, just as you do. But our people, in spite of their own need, want to share with you in your need. They've sent with me a love offering of $600 to go toward those pews."

There was a pleased murmur in the church, with a "halleujah," a few "amens," and one or two "praise the Lords" when Paul presented the check to Reverend Brown.

∽∾∽∾∽∾∽∾∽∾∽∾∽

Paul sat in his office on the third floor of the Lamb's building, praying about the coming week. The First Church of the Nazarene of Bethany, Oklahoma, had contacted him earlier about speaking at their youth camp. He had recalled his trip of a year ago where he had used the seed faith concept for deciding on his family vacation. It had cost him a week and some inconvenience. He was thinking about July in Oklahoma—"the hottest time of the year in the hottest place on earth"—someone had kidded, but the line had more truth than humor. Besides the heat and humidity, Oklahoma had chiggers, small insects that burrow under the skin of their victims and cause major discomfort.

"Surely you can't leave?" one of his staff asked him. "I mean, what happens if you're gone? They're coming to shut off the electricity at nine A.M. Thursday!"

"I know they are. But I'm not sure what to do."

"They'll understand if you cancel your trip."

"That's not the point. Here's the problem. Do we trust God to handle this for us? Or are we going to sit around and wring our hands? We've done everything humanly possible—short of selling the Lamb's—and now it's in God's hands. He knows we need the $23,000 for Con Ed and another $4,000 for current bills. If we don't have electricity, we'll have to sell. For those who keep saying 'sell,' this is the fleece. If God wants us to sell and get out, then He will have to tell us by shutting the place down! I'm going ahead with my trip to Oklahoma."

Paul left LaGuardia on Monday and began a week of speaking at the church camp in Oklahoma, all the while praying that somehow God would deliver them with a miraculous $27,000.

ᘓᔢᘓᔢᘓᔢᘓᔢᘓᔢᘓᔢᘓᔢᘓᔢ

On Wednesday evening, the Manhattan Church was having its regular midweek prayer and Bible study service. At Paul's request, a "prayer chain" had been formed earlier so that there would be around-the-clock petitions to God on behalf of the Lamb's. Now they met for corporate prayer, continuing to ask for a miracle.

During the service, the lights went out.

In the blackness, someone said disgustedly, "What a rotten trick. Man, Con Ed could have waited."

"Yeah," cried another, "we were supposed to have until nine tomorrow morning before they turned off the electricity."

"Wait, look out the window," someone called out in the dark. "The whole Times Square area is out. It's a blackout!"

Not only Times Square, but the entire island of Manhattan, the buroughs of Queens, Brooklyn, the Bronx—all of New York, parts of New Jersey, Connecticut, and areas as far north as Canada were suddenly without electricity.

At nine o'clock Thursday morning the electricity was off at the Lamb's. But no one else in New York had power or lights either. Of course, in the confusion to restore power, the order to shut off the electricity at the Lamb's was forgotten.

Friday morning, with order and power finally restored, Paul called in for a report.

"You're not going to believe this," Jim Hullinger told Paul. He went on to explain the dramatic turn of events, saving the best news for last. "And we just heard from Spiegel—they went for the pin idea und placed an order for one hundred thousand copies of the 'God Loves You' pin. Mr. Hoving has a check for us for $25,000!"

"Praise God!" Paul said, his voice breaking.

"But that's not all," Jim bubbled. "We got a letter from Rev. Roy Brown over in Brooklyn. His church took up a love offering for *us*—and sent a check for $2,000. We have exactly $27,000! I can't believe it!"

Forty-Six

B Y THE FALL of 1977, a second check from Tiffany & Co. came in time to ease the financial pressures. This time it was for $50,000 in commissions earned from the sale of pins to a Bible society. A second Spiegel commission check for $25,000 and a third for $22,500 came by year's end. The Spiegel campaign was "blessed of God" as Walter Hoving had predicted. Nearly three hundred thousand pins were sold with merchandise, giving the firm what Hank Johnson called, "Our best fourth-quarter business ever. And we must attribute it to the pins."

During their earlier financial crisis, in an attempt to find additional funds, Micki and Becki Moore had persuaded Noel Paul Stookey (of Peter, Paul, and Mary) to do a concert at the Lamb's. The Moore's, formerly from Chicago where Micki had served as art director for InterVarsity's *His* magazine, were now living in New York and were members of Paul's church. They were a folk-singing duo and were recording a gospel music album in Stookey's studio in Maine when they told him of the Lamb's and it's needs. He agreed to do a benefit concert where all the proceeds, including his fee, would go to the Lamb's.

The event proved to be a double-concert sell-out, and a huge success.

Before the concert Stookey sat in Paul's office chatting. He learned that the folk-singer had himself become a Christian during the last part of the sixties, at the zenith of the "Jesus Movement," and that he was interested in what Paul's church was doing, especially in the area of the arts.

Paul told Stookey of the church's plans for a New York Christian Theater Company, "as soon as the financial situation eases."

"That's interesting," Stookey replied. "That's been kind of a dream of mine, too. I'd love to see a Christian drama group developed."

Paul then told Stookey about a young man in the church, Van Craig, who had developed a concept of puppets designed on the basis of Renaissance art. "He calls it *Rex Magnifico* and we'd like to put it on this Christmas," Paul explained. "It's absolutely incredible. It's a nativity play, with elaborate costumes, sets, and of course, the puppets."

"That sounds exciting. What would it take to get it off the ground?" Stookey inquired.

"You mean money? I haven't even sat down to look at figures because of our cash crunch. I'm not sure." Paul looked at the quiet, humble man sitting across from him. His unassuming Christian spirit and low-key conversational tone were misleading. He was a contrast to "Paul Stookey the Performer." On stage, he was busy, vocal, laughing, singing, playing. In Paul's office, he sat quietly, with his hands folded in his blue-jeaned lap. He was silent for a moment or two, obviously thinking. Then he looked up at Paul.

"I'll give you a grant to start the New York Children's Theater. I'm especially interested in a ministry to kids . . . like that *Rex Magnifico* project. I'll provide an annual grant of $50,000 for the next five years. Let's get it going as soon as possible!"

ᴓᴓᴓᴓᴓᴓᴓᴓᴓᴓᴓᴓ

Thirty-year-old Paul Thomas finished his voice-over lines for a television commercial and left the recording studio on Fifth Avenue. A glance at his watch told him he had barely enough time to get to NBC's Rockefeller Center studios for his role in the daily soap opera *As the World Turns.* In the taxi he thumbed through the script and made sure he knew his lines. He sat back and tried to relax.

His mind went back to the strange telephone call he had gotten the night before. It was from a preacher with a Nazarene church in Manhattan, inviting him to attend on Sunday. *I was probably pretty cold toward him,* he thought.

Paul Thomas had grown up in a Nazarene church in Indiana.

So had his wife, Jan. But they had dropped out of church when they came to New York—he to search out a career in acting, she to study classical music at a New York conservatory. It wasn't as if they had turned their backs on the church. Rather, it seemed the other way around. The fundamentalist churches seemed to shut them out; there was no place there for them to express their gifts of drama and classical music.

"Rockefeller Center, buddy," the cabbie called out, bringing Paul Thomas back to the present.

The next time Rev. Paul Moore called to invite Paul Thomas to church, he responded. As soon as he came to the Lamb's, he felt at home. Before long, after several weeks of sermons and Bible study, both Jan and Paul were in regular attendance.

Jan had studied music in New York and had become a rehearsal coach with the New York City Opera Company. Then she was promoted to accompanist, and then to assistant conductor.

In addition to commercials and TV roles, Paul had appeared in stage plays on and off Broadway, including a supporting role with Jason Robards. He was one of the lucky few in New York who could claim to earn a living from acting.

The couple, now "born again" Christians, were invited to Paul and Sharon's home for Thanksgiving. After the meal, as they were sitting in the living room chatting, Paul Moore asked his guest, "Paul, you're a good actor. How do you think you could relate to the New York Christian Theater Company?"

"Whoa, wait a minute, Pastor. Jan and I may have grown up in Nazarene churches, but we didn't go to church for a long time. We dropped out of church for eight years. We're just now finding our way back," Thomas cautioned.

With cast and stage crew selected, production began for the completely original *Rex Magnifico*. Costumes made the transition from design sketches to patterns to elaborate and gorgeous reality. Sets were designed and constructed, along with the highly unique Renaissance puppets. More than nine thousand youngsters came to the Lamb's during the three-week holiday presentation. The original play and its quality production were given high media visibility during the brief seasonal run.

It was obvious to Paul that the New York Christian Theater Company was at last more than a dream. It was and would continue to be an outlet for Christian talent with hundreds of people involved in the various projects.

The Lamb's applied for and was granted an affiliation with Actor's Equity. Now they'd be listed with the other off-Broadway theaters in Manhattan and attract even wider audiences to see productions with a positive moral or Christian influence.

Paul Thomas had accepted the offer to be in charge of the New York Christian Theater Company and worked with Paul on ideas for making it a self-supporting ministry of the church.

After *Rex Magnifico* and the holidays were over, Paul began to review where the church had been and to make plans for 1978. Through Paul Stookey's grant and the Tiffany's commission checks, Lamb's Ministry Inc. was more financially secure. Paul had gone to the computer company and paid off the balance owed to them, and they had agreed to update the mailing list. Then Paul began to reactivate the newsletter and prayer-appeal mailings. Slowly, the monthly donor base began to inch up.

The staff, cut back to two people during the spring and summer crunch, was now back to sixteen.

Two major changes were taking place within the church. Its make-up was changing for one thing. Once the majority had been young singles. Then those young singles had married. Now they were beginning to have babies, and the church was having its own population explosion. These couples began to focus more on their own need as a family than on those of urban missions. They no longer had the luxury of time to devote to witnessing trips to clubs and parks.

In place of this vital evangelistic force, however, a well-trained and caring cadre of professional urban specialists became active.

Paul wondered if that was a good or bad change.

The second major change was the fact that all the major funding now came from LMI and not the denomination. A great deal of confusion and painful "we/they" feelings were still there concerning the denomination's pullout from the Nazarene Urban Missions Center.

There was so much misunderstanding on both sides that a blackout of communication still existed; Paul had not sought out contacts with the denomination, and they had not called him.

Instead, Paul discussed the technical aspects and feasibility of finding Christian men who would buy out the Nazarene interest in the Lamb's building, a plan which he felt was something that would be acceptable to most of the denominational leaders who had been urging him for over a year to sell the property.

Paul saw the disagreement as strictly a business matter, however. He was not suggesting a complete withdrawal from the Nazarenes, though there were some in the church who suggested this openly.

Forty-Seven

IN JANUARY, PAUL received a call, then a visit, from Jerry McKenna, a legal representative from the New York State Select Commission on Crime. Paul was puzzled as to why someone from a state office wanted an appointment.

"It's because of who you are and your location here in Times Square," McKenna explained. "I see what you and agencies like Teen Challenge are doing and, well, you can't argue with results. I've seen what you guys have been able to do with some of the hard-core drug addicts and runaways. That's why I'm here. You guys are our last chance."

McKenna was a stereotype of the tough New York Irish cop,

although he wasn't a law enforcement officer as such. Paul learned, however, that like most native New Yorkers, the toughness was only a veneer. Underneath was a sensitivity not yet calloused by the city's statistics, which McKenna knew so well.

"To be in Times Square is to be aware of sex," he said. "Most of it is pandering: massage parlors, X-rated theaters, the pimps and prostitutes—male *and* female." McKenna sighed. The statistics were hard to deal with in human terms. "There are one hundred thousand teenage prostitution activities in just a month's time out there. Mostly, they are little girls—thirteen, fourteen, or fifteen—being sucked into the system. They start out as runaways and get taken in by some pimp. When they're caught, they lie about their age. After a few weeks on the street as a whore a fourteen-year-old will *look* twenty-five," McKenna continued.

Paul knew something of the problem. He'd seen more than he wanted of this wasting of lives and personalities. "What can we do to help?" he asked McKenna.

"That's what I came here to ask you," he replied. "Our hands are tied. You see, Paul, the girls who *are* identified as juveniles are taken to the juvenile authorities. But they only have so much space in their detention facilities. That means they lock up the murderers, and if there's any space, they lock up the rapists or armed robbers. Sometimes. But you can count on this: The 'ordinary' muggers, thieves, and prostitutes are turned out on the street. Because prostitution isn't as serious a crime as murder, it sometimes has to be overlooked. If you've only got room to lock up one lawbreaker, it'll be the one who's potentially most harmful to society."

"Sounds pretty hopeless," Paul suggested. "But I'm assuming you have an idea, or you wouldn't be quoting these figures to me."

"That's right," McKenna grinned. "We'd like you to open up the Lamb's as a facility for female juvenile prostitutes. It'd be a minimum security facility, and we'd coordinate this with you through our offices, the family court, and the city social services department."

"Why us?" Paul asked.

"You're our last resort," McKenna admitted. "I don't know if this fits in with the Lamb's goals and purposes, but I hope so. If I was a praying man, I'd pray you'd do it."

"Well," Paul smiled, "we're praying people, and we'll pray about it and give you an answer as quickly as we can."

~~~~~~~~~~~~~~~

Mike Christensen was about two blocks from the office on his way to lunch when two boys, about ten and eleven, approached him on the street. Mike had seen them panhandling up the block. It was such a commonplace scene in Manhattan that only tourists took notice anymore. Every street had its hustlers and panhandlers. If a straight request for "spare cash" didn't get a reaction, the second try was usually more effective. It varied between a veiled threat of using a hidden knife or gun, or some similar use of intimidation. Or, if the person seemed right, the offer would be the exchange of sexual favors for "spare cash."

When Mike had first come to Times Square, the panhandlers were generally older—"hippie" types in their late teens or early twenties. Now, just a few years later, they were youngsters—boys as young as ten and girls as young as twelve.

"Hi, guys, what's happening?" Mike called out to the boys cheerfully.

"Spare cash, mister," was the answer. It sounded more like a demand than a request. The bigger boy, wearing a dirty windbreaker, had his hand stuck in a pocket that jutted out, as if he had some kind of weapon.

"Tell you what; how about if you guys join me for lunch. I'm not going to give you money, but I'll buy you a hamburger, fries, and a Coke; deal?"

They nodded, then walked across the street to a hot dog place. Mike watched them devour the food. "When did you guys eat last?" he asked.

"Yesterday . . . noon," the younger boy answered.

"Are you guys brothers?" Mike questioned.

"No . . . just friends."

"Do you live around here?" Mike continued.

"Are you a cop?" the older boy asked suspiciously.

"No," Mike grinned, "I just care about you two and wonder how a couple kids like you make out here in Times Square."

"We get by," the older one was doing the talking now.

"Panhandling?"

"Sometimes," the boy said between gulps of hamburger. "Other times we hustle tricks."

"You mean prostitution?" Mike asked.

"Sure, we get enough to live on that way."

"But . . ." Mike suppressed his outrage in order to find out more about their lives. "Do you go mostly with women or men?"

"Men. Usually gays. New York's got plenty of queers, all right," the boy laughed. He had a hard cynicism in his voice that went beyond his years.

"What about your parents?" Mike asked.

The boy swore, then answered. "I ain't never seen either one sober a day in their life. Don't even know if he's my ol' man or not. He's never home anyway. An' my ol' lady kicked me out. She told me she didn't have no money to buy food." He shrugged.

"But you get money from prostitution . . . what do you do with it?"

"Oh, maybe we get two bucks or five bucks. It's only enough to eat and go to a show. We got to a movie and sleep there," the boy explained.

When the boys finished eating, Mike explained that he was from the Lamb's and presented Jesus Christ to them. They listened and asked a few questions. Mike was always amazed to see a God consciousness on the part of the street people. *You'd think if anyone had a reason to deny God's existence, they would,* he thought, *yet, they seem to sense Him. God, help me get through to them.*

After witnessing to the boys, Mike gave them one of his business cards. "Come and look me up when you need a friend," he told them.

When they left, he looked down at his lunch, still uneaten. He wasn't hungry anymore. Part angry and part sad, Mike paid his bill and headed back to the Lamb's, wishing there was something more positive and real he could do for the children of the street.

Robin was a fourteen-year-old, going on twenty, who lived in the hotel next to the Lamb's. Paul had seen her once in a while, usually at the same "station." Robin liked to stand in the bright lights of the Hudson Theater marquee. With the warmer spring weather, her outfit was always the same: satin hot pants, heels, and a tight, tapered blouse. She stood there until a car cruising by would slow and stop. Then Robin would bend over the car, her head inside the window, and talk with the driver.

Sometimes she'd climb inside the car and the "john" would drive away. A little later he'd drop her off across the street from the Lamb's. Once in a while, a driver would merely park a half block away from the marquee where the lights weren't as bright. Then Robin would climb in the front seat and perform oral sex with the man. The jaded New York passersby merely looked the other way.

On some occasions, Robin took customers up to her room at the hotel. These were not always the typical "dirty old men" usually associated with prostitution. These were affluent, suburban businessmen in three-piece suits . . . many who even had daughters Robin's age.

Now, blank-faced and edgy, she tried to make her nightly quota of "tricks."

Paul, looking down on the street from his office, prayed silently for Robin and the sick-minded men who had to have sex with a child. Robin had stopped by the Lamb's several times. Lisa, Paul's secretary, found her in the lobby one day, looking lost and lonely. Robin admitted to Lisa that she was a prostitute but said that some day she would give it up.

One night in desperation Robin had called Paul at home. "My pimp, Bobby, beat me up because I couldn't turn enough 'tricks' tonight. I'm tired of this, Reverend Moore. I am going to kill myself!"

Paul called Joe Colaizzi and one of the women resident interns and asked them to check on Robin. She hadn't killed herself, but she didn't want to leave Bobby either.

Thinking about Jerry McKenna's words about juveniles, Paul knew that having her arrested for prostitution wouldn't help.

She'd be turned back on the street without questions. He began to think seriously about McKenna's proposal.

Mike Christensen knew the girl was probably a prostitute. Usually he avoided witnessing to girls without a female staff worker present. The girls might not understand the approach otherwise. But something made Mike change his mind this time.

"Hi, I'm Mike," he said with a smile. "I see you standing here every night when I come home from work."

"Hi, Mike . . . looking for action?"

"Uh . . . no. Just some small talk. Is that okay?"

"Sure," the girl replied. "I'm Julie."

"You live around here, too, Julie?"

"Yeah," she said in a noncommittal voice.

"Well, see you around, Julie," Mike said.

On the way home each night, Mike tried to build trust with Julie through their casual conversations. As long as he didn't interfere with business, Julie was tolerant and would talk.

"I used to go to a Baptist church," she told him, "back in Tennessee. I ran away when I turned sixteen, though. I've been in New York a year."

"How long have you been a prostitute?" Mike asked.

"Ever since I got off the bus at the Port Authority Terminal. I didn't have any money and this nice guy, dressed real fine, offered me a place to stay and to feed me until I got a job."

"And he was a pimp," Mike said cynically.

Julie shrugged. "I'd have done it eventually anyhow. It's the only way to survive."

"Don't you miss your church, and God?" Mike asked. "Wouldn't you like to get out of this and get straightened out with God?"

"Yeah," Julie said wistfully, "but not tonight. Maybe tomorrow . . . or maybe I'll come to your church Sunday. But not tonight. . . ."

The next night Mike looked for the pretty little girl with the Tennessee drawl on the way home from work, but Julie was missing. That wasn't too unusual, though. She might be with a customer. But she wasn't there the next day either, or the rest of the week. Mike never saw Julie again. He had all kinds of questions. Did she go back home? Or, more likely, was she beaten and murdered by her pimp or by some sex-crazed pervert? Had she overdosed on drugs and died in some alley? Mike knew that he'd probably never know.

Seeing Robin, their fourteen-year-old prostitute neighbor, talking with Lisa in the lobby, Paul was reminded that he was to call his friend, Dr. Sam Mayhew, in California. Dr. Sam was a member of Dr. Lee's Nazarene Church in Pasadena and a clinical psychologist specializing in juvenile problems. He had written an entire government policy and procedure manual on the topic for HEW.

"Sam? Paul Moore in New York, how are you?" Paul said cheerfully when his friend answered. He spent five minutes outlining the idea Jerry McKenna had talked to him about, and the staff's desire to do something at the Lamb's about the problem of teenage prostitution.

"We've got the people, Sam, but we need professional guidance on setting up a girls center. We need a sponsoring director, with the kind of credentials you have, to come and set this thing up," Paul said. "Can you do it?"

After praying about it, Dr. Mayhew accepted Paul's offer. At his own expense, he flew some eight times from Los Angeles to New York in order to research the need and write a proper program. Then he developed a manual and trained Lamb's staffer, Bob DiQuattro, to head the Girls' Crisis Center.

Paul and the staff, in a four-day retreat, carefully planned an "I care" rally to raise funds for the program and scheduled it for May 14. In about six weeks the new ministry would open its doors.

SHEPHERD OF TIMES SQUARE

A week later, a noisy crowd gathered in the alley outside the Lamb's. A delivery man had called the police after discovering a body while making an early morning stop at the hotel.

Paul and the staff learned the details from the newspaper.

The body of an unidentified young girl, believed to be about fourteen, was found in the alley beneath a hotel window from which she had jumped or fallen. The police suspect foul play. The girl was identified by a hotel desk clerk who knew her only as 'Robin.' She had a police record of over ninety arrests on prostitution charges, using false names, and giving her age from eighteen to twenty-six. None of the arrests, however, had her real name. It is believed 'Robin,' if that was her real name, was a runaway. It is likely her parents do not know she is dead."

Paul felt sick and angry. The girl was gone. They had not been able to reach her. More than likely she had been beaten and thrown from the upper-story hotel window by her pimp because she had threatened to leave him.

Paul slammed his fist on his desk in a rare display of emotion and threw the newspaper in his wastebasket.

~~~~~~~~~~~~~

Trish, a young teen prostitute, had lived on Staten Island in a fairly well-to-do, middle-class home. Yet, at sixteen, she had problems at home and ran away to work the streets on Delancy.

As she leaned against the side of a building in the late afternoon sun, Trish looked bored and tired. A truck honked and she moved out of the alley to the sidewalk so the driver could pull in and unload.

"Hey, mister . . . I need some money. Twenty bucks for your favorite way, okay?" she teased.

The burly driver got down from his cab and looked at her.

"Sorry, honey," he said softly, "I've got kids older'n you. What d'ya wanna be a prostitute for?"

She shrugged and walked back to her doorway.

The truck driver turned to do his duties, then paused. He remembered watching the local TV news last night. The story told of a new work in Manhattan for young prostitutes and runaways. *What was it called?* he asked himself. The Lamb's. He remembered it's location, too.

"Hey," he called to the girl.

"Change your mind, mister?" she asked coyly.

"No . . . but listen. There's this place I know about. It was on TV last night. They just opened a place for girls like you who want to get out of prostitution. If you'll go, I'll take you there," the truck driver promised. Curious, Trish decided to check out the Lamb's. She thought that if she didn't like it, she could always go to nearby Times Square and hustle. Trish got in the truck and they drove to the Lamb's.

Bob DiQuattro and the women in charge of the girls showed Trish love and affirmation she'd never had before. After several visits to the Lamb's, Trish suddenly decided to participate in the counselling program. Bob recommended that she live with an aunt until professional counsellors could help her deal with the guilt, fear, and alienation between Trish and her parents.

Slowly, over months, Trish recovered from the trauma of having sex with hundreds of unknown men. She received Jesus Christ as her Savior, and God washed the guilt away as if it were dust.

In her attempt to regain her lost innocence, Trish often sat on the floor when the girls were having Bible study, her knees up to her chin, and her arms locked securely around a teddy bear.

Bob brought to Paul some poems Trish had written that revealed some of the scars of her past life. She was forgiven and restored in God's eyes, but there was something she could never reclaim. She called it *Crucifixion of Innocence.*

Crucifixion of Innocence

My eyes are dark, I cannot see.
Innocence gone—is there no hope?
Anger and bitter confusion has left me
         . . . alone.

SHEPHERD OF TIMES SQUARE

There will be no comfort or joyful intrusion.
I cannot speak what I feel.
Is it a nightmare or just an illusion?
My past is gone—my future already sold—
    traded for cheap imitations I thought
    were gold.
Love was never there—oh, how
                 ... cold.

This world has killed me.
Now, I fall too soon ... old ... detached ...
    what was, that will be, I cannot see.*

Crucifixion of Innocence. Used with author's permission.

V. Whole People

Forty-eight

A S THE LAMB'S BEGAN to reach out with significant new
ministries in addition to continuing the ongoing ones, Ron
Mercer and others in the congregation pressed for greater accountability and organization. In the past Paul's approach to the
ministry had been instinctive and creative, and the church was
not always run like a well-oiled machine. The squeaks and
breakdowns usually resulted from funding problems.

Paul had been the spiritual leader of the church, and of
paramount concern to him was it's effectiveness in spiritual
matters. Fund raising was not his favorite priority, but his disas-
trous experiences of the last few years had forced him to become
more involved in these areas as well. He learned that in order to
do the work of the Lord, he had to have money. Without it the
work had several times come to a halt when cash shortages
forced staff reductions. Paul was now determined to become a
more effective business leader as well as minister.

Paul began to apply time management skills and decisions to
the Lamb's. The resulting organization slowly began filtering into
every area. The staff was directed to use Day Timer daily
diaries to keep track of appointments and results. These gave
Paul and other leaders a more accurate idea of how time was
spent. Those on staff with the more creative and casual attitudes
toward organization resisted the plan as "taking the heart out of
the ministry," but Paul helped them to see his plan from a
viewpoint of stewardship and accountability.

In the Spring of 1978, Paul's own outlook—and ultimately
that of the Lamb's ministry—concerning the true meaning of

Jesus' gospel was influenced by one of America's best-known clergymen.

Paul had first met William Sloane Coffin, pastor of the prestigious Riverside Church in New York City, when the two men had participated in a radio debate on what it means to be a born-again Christian. In spite of their wide differences in theology, they had become friends.

Wanting to discuss some matters, Paul had arranged an appointment with Bill Coffin, and on the day of Paul's visit, he found that Coffin had just conducted the funeral for John D. Rockefeller. The main sanctuary was filled with white carnations, whose heady fragrance greeted Paul as soon as he entered. The funeral and burial services were over now, however, and Bill Coffin was just taking off his clerical robe.

They talked for two and a half hours. Despite their opposite views, Coffin and Paul accepted each other and conversed on a common level.

"Our problem, as liberals," Coffin remarked, "is that we have social action, but without the gospel or evangelistic ferver. And your problem as conservatives is that you're *all* gospel and evangelistic ferver and no social action. Imagine what would happen if one of God's men came up with a program that was true to the gospel but also prompted by social needs and action."

Paul thought about it. It was exactly what his friend, Tom Nees, of Washington, D.C., had told him. Tom had left a typical, traditional Nazarene church in the nation's capital in order to minister to the needs of the city's black ghetto. He and his wife had moved into the "riot corridors" of Washington and had begun a program of evangelistic purpose and outreach coupled with a social conscience. Paul, in fact, had taken the train several times to Washington to see first hand what the concept was and how it worked. He had decided it had significant practical application to the streets of New York.

Based on Bill Coffin's remarks and his exposure to the work of Tom Nees, Paul became aware that in his own dealings with people, he needed to relate more to the "whole man" if he was going to respond honestly to the words of Jesus in Matthew 25.

There Jesus declared that when the hungry, the thirsty, the strangers, the sick, the unclothed, and the prisoners are cared for, He is cared for as well.

Paul realized that the Manhattan Church needed to complement its fervor for evangelism with an equal effort to see the physical and social needs of people met. This concept was presented to the congregation, and before long, volunteers were active in a number of flourishing people-centered programs that were addressing social needs, but doing so with a gospel emphasis.

A special event at Thanksgiving typified the new concern for the "whole man." Led by Joe Colaizzi, the Lamb's sponsored an elaborate Thanksgiving dinner for needy street people. Limousines were sent out to find "guests" and when they arrived, a doorman helped them from their cars and ushered them into the building. The eyes of the puzzled derelicts and down-and-outers opened wide when they saw the candle-lit banquet room with formally dressed waitresses and waiters standing ready to serve them. The dinner was not of the soup-kitchen variety but rather a sumptuous feast. To the wonderment of those in attendance, there was no "catch," and as they enjoyed the music entertainment and a short message, many of them experienced, perhaps for the first time, a full expression of Christian love and concern. An invitation was given, and a number of the street people prayed to receive Christ.

Joe Colaizzi and Jim Hullinger learned that one of the women at the dinner, Mrs. Rosen, had been "fleeced" by an unscrupulous attorney and had lost her apartment. With no money, she was forced to live in an unheated, condemned building with no food or facilities. The Lamb's staff people took her to the district attorney's office for legal redress and to other social agencies for other assistance.

Mrs. Rosen was Jewish, but she saw the love of Christ in church members' lives and soon received Jesus as her Messiah and Lord.

Joyce and Steven, the "miracle marriage" of a former prostitute and an ex-homosexual, were a demonstration not only of God's redeeming, cleansing grace, but of His capacity to redeem even the wasted years.

God used Steven and Joyce to minister to others who had problems with which the couple could relate. Once they witnessed to a homosexual who received Christ and completely severed his homosexual and transvestite lifestyle. The man was restored to church fellowship and reunited with his family. The young couple saw that their experiences could be used by the Lord in bringing others to Himself.

As if that were not miracle enough, God blessed them further. Little Molly Marie was born to the couple, completing their hopes and ideals in ways beyond their dreams or understanding.

Forty-nine

THE MEMBERS OF the New York Christian Theatre Company had an idea that would help the theater become more financially independent and at the same time bring people to the Lamb's.

"Once people come, we can tell them about our work and invite them to church here. It could be very effective as pre-evangelism," Glen Davish, one of the actors, explained to Paul.

"What's your idea?" Paul asked.

"To do an off-Broadway production of *Godspell*," he replied. "As you know, Pastor, that play ran eight or nine years on Broadway. It had a wide base of appeal with audiences and was a huge box office success. Even when the production was about to close, there were still over a thousand people at every performance."

"And you think it might be successful again?" Paul asked.

Glen was enthusiastic. "I think we will pack our theater out. It's a great play to act as a bridge to the New York theater-going public—to give them a chance to know us and give us a chance to witness to them. And it's one of very few productions that we feel is compatible with our Christian message. It's a wholesome show with all the lyrics taken from Scripture."

Paul gave the go-ahead and the musical went into production. It opened with a planned run of two weeks. But it was as popular as Glen and the others had said it would be. The theater played to standing-room-only crowds for five weeks. The extreme popularity meant additional income for the Lamb's, not only through ticket sales, but in increased business in the Sanctuary Restaurant.

The media reviews of the musical were excellent, calling the Lamb's production of *Godspell* "the sharpest off-off-Broadway show."

But after the five weeks, Paul received a call from Reverend Scutt. "Paul, I need to talk to you. It's about that musical you're putting on there! It has to end immediately."

"But why? What's wrong?"

"Is it true that you're presenting something called *Godspell*?"

"Yes, but what . . .?"

"I have received a complaint against you," Reverend Scutt told him. "It's serious, Paul. It could lead to revocation of your preaching credentials if we don't clear it up right away!"

Paul was speechless, and then angry. "What *is* this? What's going on?"

"A district pastor came to your *Godspell* play along with a group of his people. He told me he was absolutely shocked and ashamed. 'To think that they portray my Jesus as a clown in a Superman T-shirt!' he told me," Reverend Scutt continued.

"But he missed the whole point," Paul tried to explain. "That's not what . . ."

Reverend Scutt went on, "He told me the play bordered on blasphemy. Paul, if there's a reasonable explanation to this, you'd better help us find some answers. Meanwhile, I want you to close down that play." Paul's superior in the denomination was once again caught in the middle of a misunderstanding.

Paul was already on thin ice with denominational leaders because of a previous incident. Since Paul was both the pastor of Manhattan Church and president of the Lamb's, he had violated a Nazarene church rule prohibiting such an arrangement. The District Board of Orders had told Paul earlier that he would have to resign his position with the Lamb's or they would not ordain him. Being ordained meant a great deal to Paul, but he didn't feel he could leave the Lamb's before the complete organization was finished. He had refused to resign.

Several denominational meetings had been held to determine if Paul should be reprimanded. Now, because of the *Godspell* complaint, Paul was facing even more potential difficulty with his church superiors.

Paul ended the performances of *Godspell* and then waited in agony for two weeks to learn the board's decision. Finally, a district leader came with Reverend Scutt to Paul's office with the verdict. Paul listened as the men formally recited many specific grievances, among them the *Godspell* issue.

"Paul," Reverend Scutt began, "we've gone through financial crises and have had our misunderstandings. But this is no doubt the worst situation that's come up."

For the next three hours Paul was admonished. Finally, after much tense discussion on both sides, Reverend Scutt still felt caught in the middle of a problem that seemed impossible to untangle. Reluctantly he voiced his decision. "I've come to the conclusion, Paul, that you lack the authority and influence to continue here. I think it's best for you to move on to another district. I've decided not to reappoint you when your license expires. This is what the board recommended and I agree. I'll help every way I can to relocate you in another district, another city. And we have an offer to sell the Lamb's building for one million dollars, so we're going to do it."

The men told Paul that the *Godspell* incident, plus his refusal to submit to authority, were the reasons.

It was an ugly time for Paul. He was stunned and couldn't

believe what he was hearing. All he could hear was that he was a failure ... had questionable spiritual qualities ... was an egomaniac with un-Christian motives. This is not what the men were saying, but in what seemed to Paul to be a one-sided barrage, this is what *he* heard. All he understood was that everything he had worked for over the past six years was being wrenched away.

ᘛᘚᘛᘚᘛᘚᘛᘚᘛᘚᘛᘚᘛᘚ

For two sleepless days and nights, Paul reflected, prayed, and agonized. In his heart he knew his own motives. And in his mind, he couldn't think of anything he would have done differently.

A rumor began to circulate: "Paul Moore is leaving." People began to call the district office voicing sentiment on both sides of the matter. Again the church and district were polarized as the local body rose to the support of their pastor.

Sharon took the news even harder than Paul. She was more upset, angry, and hurt than he was. Sharon had always been close to Paul in his struggles. Although she had not been with Paul during the many "discussions" he'd had with district leaders, his haggard, wounded look when he came home at two or three in the morning was soon reflected in her own worried expression. They suffered together.

Hoping to find a rest from the pressure and tension, Paul and Sharon decided to spend some days at Philmont, a retreat house recently purchased by the Lamb's in rural New York as a place for its leadership to go for retreats and staff planning. Sustaining him during this personal and private hell was the love and support of Sharon and the inner assurance and affirmation that God had always before led him through miracle after miracle.

ᘛᘚᘛᘚᘛᘚᘛᘚᘛᘚᘛᘚᘛᘚ

Paul thought he was all through. In a few days, at the Nazarene's annual district assembly meeting, it would be made public that he no longer would have a license to preach. The expected humiliation was almost too much to bear. He arrived at the meeting expecting the worst.

But unknown to Paul, a drama concerning his future was being played out behind closed doors. Dr. V. H. Lewis, the general superintendent of the denomination, had heard of the commotion in the New York district and was now gently mediating the situation. After extensive discussions, the District Board of Orders agreed to vote again on Paul's license.

The assembly meeting was about to adjourn when the announcement came: Paul Moore's license had been renewed! Paul's heart jumped at this sudden intervention on his behalf. He thanked God for yet another miracle.

This event marked the beginning of a healing between the denomination and the Lamb's. The district, as attitudes and feelings began to be restored, dissolved their governing board and gave Lamb's Ministries, Inc. permission to operate the Lamb's under the jurisdiction of the Manhattan Church board. Ron Mercer and other gifted men in the Lamb's group were appointed to oversee the entire organization.

In the process, of course, the new board decided not to go ahead with the sale of the Lamb's.

As the old feelings broke down, communications were once again restored between the Lamb's and the Nazarene headquarters. "The blackout has been lifted," Paul said with relief. Now people from whom he had been alienated were calling and old friendships were rebuilt.

Curiously, what had begun in Paul's mind as an adversary relationship between Reverend Scutt and himself also changed. Paul saw in the older man the same kind of maturity, patience, and wisdom that he'd liked in his predecessor, Jack White. Paul had prayed for a reconciliation between the Lamb's and the denomination. God answered his prayer. In addition Paul began to find in Scutt the loyalty and trust reserved only for one's closest friends.

"It's incredible how God could unravel such a mess. It's obvious to me," Paul told Reverend Scutt one day. "Satan was behind all of this. The stress we were under, the misunderstandings, the lack of communication—Satan played on all these to create division and a basic mistrust for one another."

Later, Paul reflected: *Satan has tried to frustrate us on every level, but he hasn't succeeded. We've lasted. The devil has tried to whip us with discouragement, but we've hung in there. He's tried trapping some of our people in sin, but that only has started revival. He has tried to keep us from getting the Lamb's building and tried to choke us financially, but that has just given us new evangelistic opportunities. Finally, Satan did everything possible to split us from the Nazarenes. But God brought us closer together than ever before. I know we have to be wary of Satan; he goes around like a roaring lion ready to devour us. But he's tried his best shot and failed.*

Fifty

SHARON MOORE DID not rebound as quickly as her husband from the most recent incident with the district. While Paul had been able to dismiss many of the tensions and difficulties, they continued to bother her.

"I don't care what *people* think," he often told her, "but I do care what *God* thinks. That's my motive."

But Sharon felt they had been "burned" too often, and she doubted that the troubles would ever be over. She was afraid that what had just happened would happen again.

⁌⁌⁌⁌⁌⁌⁌⁌⁌⁌

Fifteen-year-old Sheri Moore was on her way to her voice lessons. In order to get there she had a take a bus, transfer, and finish her trip on a second bus.

She stood on a street corner in the afternoon sun waiting for her bus. As she waited, a big shiny Cadillac pulled up at the curb.

The driver lowered the electric window and leaned across the seat to talk. He was dark, with the latest style apricot-colored suit. His purple satin shirt was mostly unbuttoned in front. He took off his dark glasses and smiled. His voice was soft, charming.

"You're absolutely beautiful, honey," he said.

Sheri stepped backwards and her heart skipped fearfully. She tried to ignore him.

"Don't be afraid, sweetheart. I just want to be your friend."

Sheri tried to blot out his words with prayer to her Lord. Even a young, protected Christian girl living in New York knew this man was a pimp. He did not have to tell her he was recruiting young girls for prostitution. Sheri knew, and she was frightened. Sheri kept praying. Suddenly she saw her bus and ran to get on.

She saw the pimp shrug and sigh with disappointment before driving away.

Sharon cried that night when she heard Sheri's frightened replay of the incident. Sharon was afraid. Sheri was afraid. It seemed so unfair to have to live like this.

Sharon reached for the phone.

"Hello . . ."

"Hello, is Pastor home?" a woman's voice asked.

"No, I'm sorry. He just left for an appointment."

"Okay. Thanks." *Click.*

The caller had hung up before Sharon could ask if there was any message. Slowly Sharon replaced the receiver, thinking she recognized the voice on the phone as a young woman from their church. *But why did she hang up without leaving her name or message?* Sharon felt the hair on the back of her neck stand up. *Unless she was Paul's "appointment!"* If it was the woman Sharon had been thinking of, she made no secret of her affection for her minister. Further, to complicate matters, the lady's husband was just getting started in his career and was gone much of the time.

At times when Sharon was tired and at home without Paul, she would be tempted and would fantasize that possibly Paul was involved with another woman. Sharon resented that so much of Paul's time was monopolized by "other women" with whom he had to counsel. Frequently, she could not spare the time from her family and other duties to participate in counselling sessions. She knew that many young, single women in the church looked up to Paul as sort of a "father image." But she disliked having to share her husband with others so often.

Recently these feelings had aggravated her headaches. There was a constant pressure in her head, which gave way to day-long migraines two or three times a week. Sometimes they were so bad she'd get sick to her stomach as well.

If I only had someone to talk to, she thought wishfully. *But to whom does a minister's wife talk?*

As time passed, Sharon's feelings did not change. If anything, her fears raged and jealousy began to smolder.

Relations between Sharon and Paul were strained. They argued about trifles. Sharon demanded more money for their household expenses; she became more and more convinced in her own mind that Paul was shutting her out of his life.

Paul became aware that Sharon feared that he was being unfaithful. He tried love and romance to convince her.

"Look, honey," he said, holding her face in his hands. "I promise you, there is nothing to be afraid of. I'm sure Satan would love to see a romance develop between Paul Moore and a woman in his church. It would really wreck things. None of his other plans have worked. And with God's help, I don't intend to fall for such a trick. No, sweetheart, you don't have to worry."

For several weeks Sharon and Paul did not discuss Sharon's fears concerning Paul, at least not directly. But in time they grew farther apart. Paul withdrew into his work; Sharon, however, had no such diversion to take her mind off the problem. Her thoughts teased and plagued her. Hardly a day or night passed without tears. Her headaches returned and made her ill much of the time. At night, though, when Paul was sleeping next to her, she never sensed his closeness. He seemed so far away. Inside her breast a gnawing ache developed until it became a heavy and hurting pain. Sharon's whole body seemed ready to explode.

It wasn't *just* her jealousy and fear about Paul's fidelity that bothered Sharon. It was the accumulation of many other fears and frustrations.

There were so many jobs to be done, and no one to do them. As pastor's wife, Sharon wanted the church to run well, so she did all the "un-done" jobs in the church. This was in addition to her chores of cooking, cleaning, and caring for her family. She was part of the choir, counselled women in the church and at the Lamb's office, handled projects, luncheons, and helped Paul.

She was afraid the church would not function if these tasks were not done.

At home, she was afraid that they would not have enough money. Paul prayed in mammoth amounts for the Lamb's, but his own meager salary just did not meet their expenses. Feeling that he had enough money problems with the Lamb's, Sharon did not share their own money woes with Paul, and she was left to worry about paying the bills.

In her "up-tight," busy, and fearful existence, Sharon became confused over her priorities. Now she was afraid of losing everything:

—she feared losing Paul.
—she was afraid Sheri or Cathi would be kidnapped, raped, or worse by pimps or perverts.
—she feared losing their home and possessions because of their financial problems.
—she was afraid they'd lose the Lamb's and have more trouble with the district.
—she again feared the collapse of their church.

In short, Sharon's life was ruled by nightmares.

Fifty-one

IN OCTOBER PAUL took the family to Philmont for a week-end. Summer was fading, but the air was still warm and fragrant.

It was past midnight on Saturday night and everyone had gone to sleep. Suddenly, Paul was awakened by the sound of racking sobs, a near shrieking. He froze for an instant, then realized that Sharon was not in bed and that those were her terrified screams.

Paul rushed from the bedroom and found Sharon on the landing, halfway down the stairway, her eyes dilated and rolling back in her head. She was crying hysterically.

As Paul bent to help her, out of the corner of his eye he saw their children standing fearfully at the top of the stairs. He motioned them back to their bedrooms and tried to calm his wife. He soothed, shook, yelled, and hugged her without success. She could not be calmed.

Her body convulsed with great sobs and half-screams. Paul knew instantly that it was the climax of Satan's attacks. Satan had never been more real to Paul. The enemy had found Paul's vulnerable spot. He had withstood the devil when he attacked others, the church, the Lamb's. But Satan had decided that if Paul would not be defeated through his ministry to people, then he would be defeated through his family.

"Sharon, get hold of yourself!" he pleaded. Picking her up, he half led, half carried his wife outside. Still he could not calm her. In the past, just coming to this oasis had calmed and refreshed them. Now it seemed that even the green trees crowded in, and Paul felt a suffocating cloud of depression enveloping them.

Scared and angry he looked heavenward and screamed at God. "Where are *You*? Don't you know we can't *take* any more? There's nothing left! Nothing!"

Paul wept with his wife, the grief of his frustration and rage now very real.

Nearly ten years of stress and battles with satanic forces had taken their toll. His wife was broken and he was spent.

Somehow he finally calmed Sharon, and then he brought her inside.

"Mommy isn't feeling well," he said simply to the youngsters. They seemed to understand.

As he put Sharon to bed, Paul heard his daughter, Sheri, praying in the other room with the younger children. Her voice was close to breaking as she tried to explain what was happening.

"When you build a building and you take a big stone out of the foundation, the building will fall down. And our church is like that. Satan is trying to take out Mommy and Daddy so he can wreck the whole thing. That's why we've gotta pray," Sheri said with wisdom beyond her years.

Sharon went to sleep right away, and Paul, totally exhausted, also drifted off.

The next morning as the others finished preparing for the trip to the city, Paul scribbled a brief letter of resignation. As they drove toward New York he told Sharon and the children about his plan to resign as pastor of the Manhattan Church. They all began to cry quietly. He dropped Sharon and the kids off at their home and went to the Lamb's alone. It seemed as if his world had come to an end.

••••••••••••

For some reason, Paul did not read his letter to the congregation that Sunday. He did ask for prayer for Sharon and himself concerning a most difficult problem. Somehow, he muddled through the service.

Sharon was awake when he got back home, staring silently out the window. Paul tried to talk with her, to pray with her, but her only prayer was directed heavenward in anger. "Why, God? What have I done to deserve this. I even wonder if You're *there*!"

That afternoon Paul called his friend, psychologist Sam Mayhew, in California. With the same Christian concern he had shown in developing the Girl's Center program for the Lamb's, Dr. Mayhew now listened to Paul. After hearing Paul unburden his soul, his guts, Sam suggested lovingly, "Paul, why don't you ask Sharon to come and stay with my wife and me for two weeks. The rest and warm California air will be good for her. We'll do all we can to help."

Sharon did not resist. She flew that night from LaGuardia to Los Angeles where she was to be met by Dr. and Mrs. Mayhew.

As Paul watched the plane pull away from the ramp and taxi away for take-off, he prayed wordlessly for his wife.

Paul shuffled through the early November snow that had fallen on the quiet hills of Philmont. He thought of Sharon, three thousand miles away, in a climate altogether the opposite. He missed her.

He pulled his jacket collar up and watched the steam of his breath in the cold, dry air. Paul had never felt so alone in his life. His mother and dad were dead. No one understood. There were some in his church who cared—who loved their pastor—but most had no idea what he and Sharon were going through.

Paul thought again of the letter of resignation he had written but hadn't turned in. He planned to do so soon. He knew that the Christian church doesn't allow weakness on the part of its leaders.

The shepherd must always show strength; he can never have problems, never fail as a man. It's an unwritten rule, he thought.

To admit failure or defeat would jeopardize his ability to minister. The congregation would begin to question his qualifications to lead them.

Now, shuffling through the snow on a New York hillside, his children confused, his wife in California, and no one in his church or denomination who really seemed to understand or care, Paul felt utterly helpless and alone.

He began to cry. "God," he wept, "Are You real? Or have I 'psyched' myself up over the years to believe in You? Where are You?! It even seems to me that *You've* forsaken us. Don't you even *care?*"

ᴏᴗᴏᴗᴏᴗᴏᴗᴏᴗᴏᴗᴏᴗᴏᴗᴏᴗᴏᴗᴏ

God heard and began a slow miracle of healing in both lives, though they were separated by three thousand miles. Through rest, long hours of counselling, and Christian therapy, Dr. Mayhew led Sharon back to wholeness. Her migraine headaches left, and she felt the knot of fear in her breast dissolving.

Sharon began to see that she had put layer upon layer of coverings over her problems instead of confronting and dealing with them. Growing up with an insecure and low self-image, she had unconsciously been acting out a role. She thought to be loved, fulfilled, and accepted by others, she had to live out a role of "pastor's wife," a stereotype that had nothing to do with who she was or what she wanted. If other people "expected" a pastor's wife to do or be something, she never questioned it. She even thought it was what God wanted.

It took half a month, but Sharon began to see her life, roles, and abilities in proper perspective. The road back to wholeness was ahead.

She had not remembered God's supportive love and resources that were available to her. She had forgotten the truth of Ephesians 6 when her world had come crashing down upon her.

Finally then, find your strength in the Lord, in his mighty power. Put on all the armour which God provides, so that you may be able to stand firm against the devices of the devil. For our fight is not against human foes, but against cosmic powers, against the authorities and potentates of this dark world, against the superhuman forces of evil in the heavens. Therefore, take up God's armour; then you will be able to stand your ground when things are at their worst, to complete every task and still to stand (Eph. 6:10–13).

Sharon began to pray again and found sense for her life through God's Word. The Bible never mocked her, never failed her confidence. She found God speaking to her in meaningful, personal ways:

> My brothers, whenever you have to face trials of many kinds, count yourselves supremely happy, in the knowledge that such testing of your faith breeds fortitude, and if you give fortitude full play you will go on to complete a balanced character that will fall short in nothing (James 1:2–4).

> Is anyone among you in trouble? He should turn to prayer . . . A good man's prayer is powerful and effective (James 5:13,17).

> The Lord is near; have no anxiety, but in everything make your requests known to God in prayer and petition with thanksgiving. Then the peace of God, which is beyond our utmost understanding, will keep guard over your hearts and your thoughts, in Christ Jesus (Phil. 4:6,7).

Sharon reflected on how fear and misunderstood priorities had plagued her life. She resolved to begin rebuilding by ordering her priorities: first, God; second, her husband; third, her children; fourth, her work.

If we won every person in New York City to Christ, but lost each other or lost our children because our attitudes were all wrong, I don't think it would balance, Sharon reasoned. She also suspected that perhaps the reason her prayers were not answered was because she had been asking out of wrong motives.

ᕫᕫᕫᕫᕫᕫᕫᕫᕫᕫᕫᕫ

Meanwhile, in New York, Paul was completely broken. He saw how his pride had interfered with his logic. In his utter "aloneness," Paul spent long hours and days in conversation with God. Christ became his "very present help in trouble."

"I should have been more considerate and sensitive to Sharon," he confessed to God. "Lord, forgive me for lacking the spiritual qualities I should have had," Paul cried. "I completely forgot in this whole mess the principle You taught me about marriage—that I can never be complete without Sharon—that Sharon is my best asset. Instead of yelling at her to pull herself together, I should have seen that Sharon was trying to get my attention. Forgive me, Lord . . . ."

Paul had retreated further into prayer than he'd ever gone before. Effie Jansen Canapa, somehow sensing her pastor was having trouble, gave Paul a copy of the classic book *Power Through Prayer*, by E. M. Bounds. She had underlined pertinent passages, knowing if she could get Paul praying, God would work out whatever it was that was troubling her minister.

In this book Paul read, "God's plan is to make much of the man, far more of him than anything else. Man is God's method. The church is looking for better methods; God is looking for better men."

It was exactly the principle Paul had learned earlier—"being before doing." He was reminded and rebuked. "You can't accomplish My purposes with your abilities," God seemed to say to him. "It is not through your 'promoter' qualities, but through My methods—and My method is to make you a better man. Relax, Paul. Trust Me. I am making you the kind of man necessary to accomplish My purposes."

As Paul continued to examine his life, he prayed that Sharon would forgive him and that they could erase their differences and difficulties.

At no time did Paul even think about divorce. Even when his own pride distorted his thinking, he would have done *anything* to put the pieces of his fragmented marriage back together.

Pride and arrogance, he thought. *Those are the reasons I'm lacking in spirituality.* Under conviction of guilt and his responsibility in Sharon's near emotional breakdown, Paul took inventory of his life. He promised God to do something about his lack of love and sensitivity toward Sharon.

When they were finally reunited, it was obvious to them both that God had worked His miracle. A supernatural healing had taken place—spiritual, physicial, and emotional. Paul had a new love, respect, and sensitivity toward Sharon. She had a new sense of her own personhood and no longer had to live up to someone else's expectations.

In reading Evelyn Christenson's book *Lord, Change Me,* Sharon had discovered the principle of changing other people and circumstances through the power of prayer and the willingness to make changes in oneself. She released Paul to God instead of trying to change him. In making changes in her own life, she saw Paul's life change for the better as well.

Over several months, Sharon found new love and healing she never thought possible.

She and Paul went on another retreat to nurture the new love God had awakened within them.

Sharon felt a deep inner and lasting assurance that her personal "hell" had ended. She knew in her soul that God would never require such pain from them again. She began to appreciate a new reality and truth in Romans 8:28 ". . . we know [that God] co-operates for good with those who love God and are called according to his purpose." Since it had been for *His* purpose that they had been called, she knew it was Satan who had attacked them, who had tried to drive and keep them apart. Now the agony of those satanic attacks was over. She knew that; she had God's own inner assurance. *The Scripture is right,* she thought, holding tightly to her man. *Even that wrenching, emotional hurt turned out to be "positive pain"—like the pains of childbirth—because it brought me closer to Paul and made us more in love with each other than ever before.*

Like childbirth . . . she thought and began to count the months. It was now May, 1979. Her personal agony had begun in September, nine months earlier. God had used the experience to develop a richer, more loving relationship—with Paul, her family, her church. Her life was infinitely better for these "birth pangs." Sharon recalled how the doctor had always placed her newborn infant in her arms after the delivery. At that moment, all the fears, doubt, and months of sickness and pain were forgotten. She saw God's loving analogy.

"Thank You, God . . ." she prayed, with tears of happiness

running down her face, which was already flushed in satisfied peace and total joy. It was more than her heart could hold.

Fifty-two

ON SATURDAY, MAY 5, 1979, a nervous and slightly flustered Paul Moore paced back and forth in a small office. Paul had the feeling he was reliving a part of his life. Then he remembered. Seventeen years earlier he had felt the same jitters, in this same place—the church where he and Sharon had married. It was also the church where he had been given his first license to preach exactly ten years before. Today the Lakeland Church (the Old Dover Church) in New Jersey was to be the place for Paul's ordination.

Paul sat in the office with Sharon, the district secretary, and three other ministers and their wives. The other ministers were to be ordained as well.

One of the ministers looked at Paul with great affection. There was a volume of wordless communication between the two. He was Charlie Rizzo, pastor of the New Milford Church of the Nazarene. Ten years earlier, he had been Paul's first convert, and he had been God's choice to replace Paul at New Milford. The revival, now ten years distant, was still bearing fruit. The church had continued to grow and young people were still finding Christ there.

Paul looked at Sharon who was beaming with pride and love for her husband. She hugged him and squeezed his hand as it was time for the ceremony to start.

As Paul and the others walked down the aisle during the processional, he could hardly contain his emotions.

At the front were the denominational leaders. Presiding superintendent, Charles Strickland, convened the service. At his side was Reverend H. V. Scutt, the district superintendent.

To the four ministerial candidates, Dr. Strickland smiled warmly and reviewed their progress toward this day. "Your walk toward this moment has been marked with struggle and battles," he said. "We have watched you, perhaps even at times kept you at arms' length. But it was for a purpose. You pamper only the spoiled child. You were not pampered. You had to fight through to prove your determination, to prove you really cared for your heritage."

Paul listened as Dr. Strickland challenged them not to assume that they had completed the course, had somehow "arrived spiritually." Rather he urged them to recognize the tremendous responsibility God had entrusted to them and to act upon it.

He continued, "The apostle Paul wrote to the believers at Corinth: 'Therefore seeing we have received this ministry, as we have received mercy, we faint not . . . For which cause we faint not; but though our outward man perish, yet the inward man is renewed day by day.' "*

He looked at the ministers. "You've been given a commission—to know all you can about Jesus Christ and share it with everyone else. You must know His power, His grace, His suffering. Whatever you have, you owe entirely to God's grace."

Paul's mind grabbed at the words as if they were meant only for him. God was speaking through Dr. Strickland and reminding him of His *amazing grace.* God's grace had brought healing between two polarized positions in the church, and the results had been truly *amazing.* And the healing of Sharon's fearful heart was nothing short of miraculous, and again a tribute to God's wonderful grace.

"You've been given God's grace," Dr. Strickland said, "so that you can be the agent who offers it to others who need it. Don't lose heart. Satan will come to you again. But you will understand why. Remember, 'faint not, for the inner man is

---

*2 Cor. 4:1,16, KJV.

renewed day by day.' Stay in God's Word . . . stay on your knees
. . . and love your wives and children, as unto the Lord."

At the altar following his message, Dr. Strickland laid his
hands on the first two men and ordained them into the ministry.
Then, smiling to the families and friends seated in the auditorium, he explained, "Reverend Scutt has asked for a point of
personal privilege at this time."

Reverend Scutt came over to where Paul and Charlie Rizzo
were kneeling and placed his hands upon them and prayed. It
was a terribly emotional moment for all three.

The elders gathered around to complete the ceremony.
Those who hadn't understood before, those who had fought *for*
Paul and those who had argued *against* him in the past, were
united in prayer before God. It was too much for them. Tears
could not be stopped, but neither could joy be contained.

When the service ended, Paul shook hands with all the elders
and participants. But he singled out his church superior, Reverend Scutt, for a special greeting. The two men, overpowered by
the poignant meaning of the moment, wrapped their arms
around each other in a joyful, brotherly embrace.

Fifty-two

ONE WEEK LATER it was Mother's Day.

"Poppa John" O'Shaughnessey observed this holiday, as well as his fourth year at the Lamb's, without ceremony. He shuffled up and down the stairs with his trash collector, stopping at each office to empty the waste baskets. It was his work, his ministry. And Poppa John took it seriously.

In many respects his quiet consistency and dependability went unnoticed. But many recognized Poppa John's devotion for what it was—a life of purpose being lived out in what were obviously his final years.

As he crossed the auditorium, Poppa John's childhood Catholic roots brought him to an abrupt stop. Unconsciously he bowed and crossed himself before continuing his rounds.

At nine o'clock sharp every Sunday—not before or after but always at nine—Poppa John would knock softly at the door of Paul's office. Paul, usually in prayer and making final preparations for the morning service, knew the knock.

"Come in, Poppa John," he'd call.

"Good morning, Pastor. And isn't it a lovely day?" Poppa John would smile, his light Irish accent coloring his greeting.

"It's a great Lord's Day," Paul would respond.

The ritual continued. Poppa John would hand Paul an envelope. In it would be two dollars—Poppa John's tithe to the ministries of the Lamb's. And it was every bit as important as a $15,000 check, because of what it represented. Each dollar bill was bathed in sacrifice and love.

On this Mother's Day, Poppa John showed up as usual. After he left, Paul made his final notes for the pastoral prayer, then saw that it was time to go downstairs to the auditorium. It was his second Sunday as a fully ordained minister. But he was not preaching today. The bulletin announced a special Mother's Day service.

Effie Jansen Canapa was seated at her familiar place at the piano. She had a new radiance since her Christmas candlelight wedding to a Manhattan executive.

Yvonne Mercer, seated with *Ron,* rose at the proper time to lead the singing. *"Dusty" Hullinger,* using her *Living Bible,* read the morning Scripture.

Then Paul led in the pastoral prayer and introduced the special speaker.

Sharon Moore stood in the pulpit and began the morning message. Her text was 2 Timothy 1:7: "For God hath not given us the spirit of fear; but of power, and of love, and of a sound mind" (KJV). She shared the story of her recent hurts and healing. Nervous at first, Sharon grew confident as she continued.

As Paul proudly watched his wife, he sensed that Sharon had been given a genuine anointing by the Holy Spirit that made her thoughts and words articulate and powerful.

At the conclusion of the service, Paul and Sharon stood at the door greeting people as they left. Paul's eyes ranged over the congregation.

Bob and Esther DiQuattro were there. Bob was taking a leave from his responsibilities as Director of the Lamb's Center for Girls to enroll at Yale Divinity School to become a full-time counselor and teacher.

Mike Christensen, the recent teacher at Wednesday night Bible study, was talking to Bob. He also had been accepted to study at Yale to prepare for the ministry.

Barbara Billings Bruccoleri and her husband, *Joe,* were in the service. They had taught the Manhattan Church's young marrieds' Bible class that morning.

Joe Colaizzi was just coming into the building from the Kingston Hotel where he had been preaching to a small group of elderly poor, transients, and derelicts.

Joyce and Steven, carrying baby, Molly, shook hands with the pastor and asked him to pray for them and a decision they had to make regarding a possible full-time ministry for the two of them.

John and Beverly Hillyer, good friends as well as loyal church members, kidded Paul about letting his wife preach more often.

Edsel Stenstrom, head usher for four years, and assistant to the church treasurer, finished putting the offering receipts away and came to where *Martha* was waiting. The two of them left after greeting Paul and Sharon.

Paul and Jan Thomas, along with *Joel and Maggie Tucciarone,* were among the last to leave. On her way out, Maggie handed Paul a letter. "I've been in prayer all during April and reading the Scriptures," she said. "I've put down some of the thoughts and insights God gave me."

Paul took the letter and scanned it. It was six pages of neatly penned lines, carefully and prayerfully compiled.

He glanced at the pages for highlights, planning to read it more thoroughly later at home.

Dear Paul,

I keep thinking the Lord is going to (or already has) pour out his Holy Spirit upon the Lamb's. . . .

From the Lamb's will come a great spiritual awakening in New York City . . .

Prayer and praise groups are most important. Prayer is spiritual violence against the kingdom of evil. . . .

The "fighting men" at the Lamb's are those the Lord has raised up to do battle by means of prayer and praise . . .

It doesn't take a genius to realize that Satan is upset that we are in "his" Times Square . . .

The Lord wants us to be careful how we live. He is holy and requires that His people be holy . . .

The Lord is about to pour out tremendous blessings upon us if we are obedient to Him. We must be careful not to be discouraged when we are tested, because He wants us to be strong. . . .

Her words were an affirmation of all that God had been saying to Paul lately. He thanked Maggie and folded the letter.

Sharon had gathered Sheri, Cathi, and Paul Jr. while he was glancing over Maggie's "prayer letter." Sharon waved for Paul to come.

They had reservations for a leisurely Mother's Day brunch at a nearby restaurant. It would be the fitting climax not only for the day but also for all that had happened in the recent months.

"I'm ready," Paul announced with a wide, pleased smile. "Sunday brunch to honor the best woman in the entire world—right kids?"

They all agreed.

"Let's go then, before we lose our reservation," Paul urged.

As they were walking out the door, one of the Lamb's residents ran up to them.

"Pastor! Pastor Moore—wait!"

"What is it?"

"You've gotta come with me—now. It's an emergency!"

Paul motioned for his family to wait in his office while he checked. "What's wrong?" he asked.

The man hurried Paul into the auditorium and back to the dressing room area. He opened the door and pointed inside.

Paul's mouth dropped open. In the room were a half-dozen men in various stages of undress. They were donning white, ruffled dresses as if they were a group of senoritas preparing for a gala Mexican hat dance.

"What is going on here?" Paul demanded. "Who are you?"

In broken English one of the men explained that they had rented the auditorium to present an ethnic folk festival. Unconvinced and with his anger mounting, Paul could only see that a group of men were going to present flamenco dances dressed as Spanish women.

"Out!" Paul ordered. "Get your things and leave immediately."

As Paul fumed someone else came and explained that in Spain it was traditional once a year for men to entertain their families with such an impersonation.

"I don't care what they do in Spain," Paul retorted, "you are not going to do it in our sanctuary in our church!"

There was a chorus of agrument and disagreement as the group of men claimed their legal rights to go on with the performance. "We've sold every seat. Our mothers, our wives, our friends are all coming," said one of the men wearing a dress.

"You rented the place under false pretenses," Paul charged. "We never would rent to a group like yours!"

"Discrimination!" one of the men shouted back, "We'll sue."

"So sue me. Just get out of here."

"We have tickets sold. We can't leave!"

"Yes, you can, and you *will*."

"We'll call NBC and all the networks. We'll picket in costume outside your place. You'll be on the six o'clock news! And we'll sue," a man yelled.

Paul groaned inwardly as he wondered if this incident would be the beginning of another long misunderstanding between him and others in the church family. *Well*, thought Paul, *my ordination might be the shortest in the history of the Nazarene church!*

"Happy Mother's Day," Paul muttered under his breath, as he went to send his family out to eat without him and to find the culprit who had scheduled the "folk festival."